HIMALAYAN CLIMBER

In the Western Cwm of Everest.

The Sierra Club, founded in 1892 by John Muir, has devoted itself to the study and protection of the earth's scenic and ecological resources - mountains, wetlands, woodlands, wild shores and rivers, deserts and plains. The publishing program of the Sierra Club offers books to the public as a nonprofit educational service in the hope that they may enlarge the public's understanding of the Club's basic concerns. The point of view expressed in each book, however, does not necessarily represent that of the Club. The Sierra Club has some sixty chapters coast to coast, in Canada, Hawaii, and Alaska. For information about how you may participate in its programs to preserve wilderness and the quality of life, please address inquiries to Sierra Club, 730 Polk Street, San Francisco, CA 94109.

Roger Baxter-Jones and Alex MacIntyre descending from an
acclimatisation climb on Nyanang Ri prior to their ascent of the
South Face of Shishapangma in 1982.

(*inside front cover*) The East Face of Everest from Makalu.

(*inside back cover*) Looking south-west from K2 to Masherbrum.

DOUG SCOTT

HIMALAYAN CLIMBER

A LIFETIME'S QUEST TO
THE WORLD'S GREATER RANGES

SIERRA CLUB BOOKS · SAN FRANCISCO

Library of Congress Cataloging in Publication Data
Scott, Doug K.
    Himalayan climber: a lifetime's quest to the world's
greater ranges / by Doug Scott.
        p.   cm.
    ISBN 0–87156–599–4 : $35.00
    1. Scott, Doug K.   2. Mountaineers—
Biography.   3. Mountaineering—Himalaya
Mountains—History.   4. Himalaya Mountains—
Description and travel.
GV199.92.S4A3   1992
796.5'22'092—dc20
[B]   91–46449
                                                        CIP

Colour separations by J Film Process, Bangkok

Photoset by J&L Composition Ltd, Filey, Yorkshire, UK

Printed in Italy by L.E.G.O., Vicenza
10 9 8 7 6 5 4 3 2 1

ACKNOWLEDGEMENTS The author and publisher would like to
thank the following for their help in producing this volume:
Rob Wood has been an inspiring force throughout; Margaret
Body, Andy Fanshawe, Jenny Macloed, Janis Tetlow, Sharu
Prabhu, Clive and Sue Davies, David Oswin, Ad Carter, Judy
Brownlow, Chris Bonington, Clive Rowland, Jan Scott,
Vivienne Schuster, Pip Hopkinson, Audrey Salkeld, Greg
Child and Helgi Benidiktson have all provided editorial
advice or assistance.
    Seventy-six photographs taken by others are credited below
[abbreviations – 2 (both pictures), t (top), b (bottom), l (left),
i (inset), br (bottom right), cl (centre left) etc]: Jean
Afanassieff 128(bl); Roger Baxter-Jones 130(br), 140(t and
bl); Pete Boardman 96(bl), 124(t); Chris Bonington – front
cover, back flap, 38(br), 61(t), 64(b), 66(t), 84(l), 85(tl,bl,tr);
Greg Child 110, 113(t), 115(r), 116(t), 116(br), 119(tr),
120(r), 178(b); Charles Clarke 41(tl); Peter Cox 181(b);
Clive Davies jacket – back cover (tl,cl,tr), 11(tl), 12(bl),
19(b), 24(tr,br), 57(br); Estcourt collection 124(b); Mick
Garside 22(l), 23(tl); Dennis Hennek 57(c); Rod
Hewing 12(tl); Guy Lee 21(l); Alex MacIntyre, jacket – back
cover (br), 159(tl), 159(b); Paul Nunn 68(tl), 81(t); Sharavati
Prabhu 165(tl), 169(tr), 171(bl,br), 171(br), 179(bl), 179(br),
180(l,tr), 182(br); Nick Prestcott 157(i); Chris Ralling 41(tr);
Ronnie Richards 34(b), Clive Rowland 80(b), 85(b); John
Roskelley 66(i); Galen Rowell 86(t); Robert Schauer 183(c);
Joe Tasker 96(t), 127(t,b); Pete Thexton 113(b), 121(tr); Ken
Vickers 27(tl,tr,b); Pete Warrington 20(l); Tony Watts 22(tr);
Ken Wilson 48, 48/49(c); in addition Mike Covington, Geoff
Price, Victor Saunders, David Harris, Christine Baxter-Jones,
Tom Tasker, Carolyn Estcourt, Frances Daltry, John Cleare
are thanked for their efforts in photographic research and
other photographic assistance.

A view from Nuptse over the Lhotse/Nuptse ridge to Makalu

CONTENTS

Introductory Note

Doug Scott's life is driven by a passion to climb. He is consumed by the challenge of the world's highest peaks but this has been accompanied by a geographer's fascination with visiting new places, a curiosity about the metaphysical undercurrents that accompany great risk, a need to plumb the capabilities of mind and body and a corresponding empathy with mountain peoples who confront such tests in their everyday struggle with life.

His climbing record (see page 192) lists a multiplicity of outstanding ascents from around the world, most notably major new routes on three of the world's highest mountains. It places Scott in the front rank as one of the world's most innovative Himalayan climbers. What Chris Bonington has achieved in terms of single-minded organisation and drive, or what Reinhold Messner has demonstrated by his speed and panache have been matched by Doug Scott's determination always to try for something different and never be satisfied by the more obvious and easier routes to success.

This book provides a comprehensive photographic portrait of his remarkable climbing career (an autobiography follows). Scott has assiduously photographed his travels and has always had enough strength to record the critical moments of the highest climbs, thus capturing some of the best high-altitude photographs ever taken. But though the pictures reflect the splendour and danger of the great peaks, they may fail fully to convey the challenge of the environment in terms of wind, low temperature and rarified air pressure. Those seeking authenticity would have to leaf through the book in a wind-blasted, refrigerated decompression chamber, in full climbing gear with a heavy rucksack and working a treadmill, all in an atmosphere adjusted to one third normal sea-level density. In the earlier Himalayan books, or in accounts of space travel, sub-aqua or cave-diving, the hostility of the environment is obvious from the complexity of the technical equipment being used. Modern high-altitude climbing provides no such emblems, so that in the pictures the summit of Kangchenjunga (8598m) could easily be mistaken for the top of Ben Nevis on a fine winter's day. There is no hint that the body chemistry could fail at any moment. Above 7500 metres climbers who eschew bottled oxygen play a deadly physiological game where the penalty for miscalculation, while usually not immediate, can be terminal. Even then progress is slowed to a snail's pace, and the capacity for logical judgement is also impaired. Carrying any weight (tents, food, fuel, sleeping bags and equipment) makes the task immeasurably greater.

Today's Himalayan climbers must therefore have immense strength and vitality, must acclimatise very carefully, should be fully skilled and experienced, must be alert to danger, yet hardened enough not to be critically frightened (and mountains are very frightening places) by any unexpected trauma, be patient during storms, determined in attack and wise in retreat, be diplomatic and good team players, be compassionate but sometimes have a touch of selfishness. With these qualities they will be fully prepared for the big trial, but they must also know themselves in the deepest sense – 'to be in touch', as Scott frequently mentions, 'with that critical inner voice'.

A great Himalayan climb draws on the deepest resources of body and mind. It can lay bare the climber's weaknesses and strengths. It can in turn humble and elate. Its fascination may be because it exemplifies mankind's continuing need for trial by fire, that quest for the ultimate human test. Doug Scott has been there often over the past three decades. This book provides some hint of insight into *his* quest of self-discovery.

KEN WILSON, 1991

In Great Danger in a High Place

My early years in Britain and the Alps

I

The gritstone edges of Derbyshire, Staffordshire and Yorkshire are now recognised (in international terms) as a unique climbing ground. They provide thousands of short satisfying climbs that preserve a quality of challenge in every grade where pitons have always been shunned. I was lucky to begin my climbing on grit and I believe it inculcated a combative instinct when dealing with problems on rock as well as a lifelong enjoyment of handjamming – it was a valuable apprenticeship that I have in common with generations of British climbers.

In the late fifties we were all very much in awe trying to repeat the great gritstone routes established by Joe Brown and Don Whillans. One of my best early leads was The Sloth (*left*) on the Staffordshire Roaches, one of Don's most celebrated routes. Majestically sited at the apex of one of the finest edges, the climb, though diminutive and no longer considered difficult, still exudes a powerful challenge. These days it is well protected with nut runners but when Don led it in 1955, and also when I repeated it in 1961, we relied only on slings draped over spikes below and above the roof. (This 1968 ascent, with George Jones belaying, shows the improved protection provided by nuts.) Such early graduation routes led naturally to far sterner tests such as The Dangler (Stanage) and the fierce Emerald Crack on Chatsworth Edge which gave me my hardest early gritstone lead.

A fortune-teller told my mother, just before she and my father married, that she would have three sons and the eldest would be in great danger in a small shelter in a high place with all the world watching. In 1975, after Dougal Haston and I had climbed Everest, we were forced to share an improvised bivouac just below the summit. It taught me a lot about survival and the bounds of the possible at altitude and it allowed my mother to stop worrying quite so much every time I set off for a big climb.

I would not however claim this as evidence that I had been predestined for climbing. Like many others of my generation I drifted into it by chance, helped in my case by the freedom my parents gave me to explore my immediate environment on the edge of Nottingham, across fields and into the woods, climbing trees and making dens. During an outing in Derbyshire with the Boy Scouts we visited the Black Rocks at Cromford. Our scout master would not let us onto the rocks although there were men there linked together with new white ropes snaking up the cracks and chimneys, barking commands to each other like soldiers. Three of us were inspired enough to cycle out from Nottingham the following weekend armed with an old tow rope and my mother's washing line. We slithered and slipped, grazing our bare legs, but managed to climb the easier chimneys. That was in the spring of 1953. A few weeks later Hillary and Tenzing got to the top of Everest on my twelfth birthday.

During those early years we survived many tricky situations, but we learnt from our mistakes and by watching what experienced climbers were doing.

In 1955 Mick Garside and I caught a bus to Llandudno and walked south over all the Carnedds to climb for a week on and around Tryfan. Holidays in the Lake District and Scotland naturally followed. Our school had an enlightened head who sent us off to the recently opened White Hall Outdoor Pursuits Centre, and in school time. It was there our horizons were widened by meeting our early heroes, Geoff Sutton and Harold Drasdo, and being enthralled by Gordon Mansell's tales of Joe Brown, the human fly, on Cenotaph Corner with his second unconscious from a dropped peg hammer or hand-jamming his way up a crack above 8500m on Kangchenjunga. They were all great characters at White Hall in those days, full of enthusiasm for climbing and all of life and, wanting to be part of it, Mick and I managed to inveigle our way in for a period as temporary instructors with all expenses paid.

The usual winter weekend pattern became a journey by bus to the Peak, then

Leading Joe Brown's Peapod on Curbar Edge.

Tackling an overhang on the South Face of Torre Grande in the Cinque Torre in 1962, a short Dolomite climb much valued as a training route before tackling bigger things on the Tofana and the Tre Cime. Note the step etriers and kletterschühe footwear.

kipping in barns or bivving under boulders on the Edges. There were bacon and grit butties for breakfast and a big stew reeking of paraffin for dinner. On Sunday evenings we had a stiff walk from the Edges down to Bakewell and then back on the bus singing and shouting the odds in the steamy interior, backs of hands stinging from gritstone grazes and smelling of lichen.

I naturally climbed with an ever-widening circle of friends from the Nottingham area. I never did get to climb the hardest routes of the day, partly because I was not as naturally talented, and partly as a result of my interest in hill walking and playing rugby football. By 1961 there were enough of us to form the Nottingham Climbers' Club, mainly to organise bus trips to Wales and the Lake District. At that time our regular weekend climbing was on the limestone cliffs near Matlock in the Derwent Valley – High Tor, Wild Cat Tor and Willersley. It was there that I acquired a taste for pioneering new routes. This can be very time-consuming and the quality of the climb may not add up to much but, even so, the pleasure of investigation and discovery always remained the main spur to action. It was this simple curiosity to see what had not been seen before that was to take me much further afield to rock faces around the world and on the highest Himalayan peaks. I cannot deny that there was also a certain pleasure in seeing myself credited with having made the first ascent of some particular route and I was competitive to the extent of wanting to get onto a possible line before anyone else did, though this was more for the intrinsic interest of the route than bettering anyone else.

We were lucky to have underdeveloped limestone crags on our doorstep that gave us scope to open up routes at our own grades. In the Alps and Dolomites I mostly repeated other routes, but gained in experience and confidence that eventually enabled me to pioneer routes of my own in the remote ranges.

Many people concentrate solely on rock climbing but they are missing the equally interesting aspect of hill walking and general mountaineering. In Easter 1957 I went off with two school friends to Scotland. We walked the complete Mamore Ridge. At Sgurr Eilde Mor my companions headed back down to Glen Nevis while I continued as I still had a surplus of energy, being very fit from cross-country running and rugby. I set off up to Stob Choire Claurigh and then walked back along the Grey Corries ridge to Carn Mor Dearg. The sun was warm, yet the clear air had a bite to it. There was hardly a cloud in the sky; I was surrounded by snow-covered mountains, one behind the other for miles in all directions. As I moved up the final slopes of Aonach Beag there was a marvellous moment when a huge stag appeared on the summit, surveyed the scene, then turned and ambled down the slopes towards Glen Nevis. I ran out of steam just before Ben Nevis and anyway it was getting dark, so I descended the steep slopes back to the glen. It was the best day I'd ever had in the hills and I experienced feelings of contentment that persisted for days. No other activity bore comparison. Those fourteen hours over twelve Munros were a turning point. Mountaineering then took over to the exclusion of cross-country running and athletics and each summer trips to the Alps and further ranges seemed all important.

I have climbed in many mountain ranges but I still return regularly to the Alps where, particularly in the Mont Blanc range, there is the best combination of rock and ice, sensibly proportioned, not outrageously big like the Himalaya.

It was several years before I found myself focusing in on the one big route, preferring during my early years to sample as much variety and quantity of climbing as possible from the Dolomites to Chamonix. To help pay for my

Nottingham Climbers' Club members: *(above left)* on Scafell, Christmas 1961 *(l to r)* Rod Hewing, George Jones, myself, Steve Bowes; *(above right)* at the Biolay campsite, Chamonix, 1968 Mick Terry, Brian Palmer, Ted Wells, Guy Lee and Bob Shaw.

A steep section on the North Face of the Aiguille du Plan, in the days before drooped picks when much step-cutting was required.

alpine holidays, for a few years I did two weeks guiding each season. In 1961, after guiding six Mountaineering Association clients up routes continuously for ten days, we arrived on the summit of Mont Blanc just as Don Whillans and Chris Bonington reached the same point after climbing the Central Pillar of Frêney. I couldn't help but reflect that I had just spent two weeks of fine weather guiding when I too could have got stuck into a big objective.

The one aspect of my alpine climbing that startles me now, looking back, was that every season there were incidents in which we could have been killed. After climbing my first big route, the North-East Face of the Piz Badile with Des Hadlum, I slipped in the dark on a stream-washed slab and hurtled down to a fortunate but bone-jarring halt on a ledge right on the lip of a seventy-metre vertical drop. Then there was the fierce lightning storm on the Geant with Lyn Noble, a huge chockstone rattling down a gully Brian Chase and I were in when returning from the summit of the Fou, an ice avalanche creaming a gully Bill Cheverst and I had just vacated after laboriously climbing, cutting steps, for an hour on the Aiguille du Plan North Face, rocks raining down the Dru Couloir on Dave Nicol and myself en route to the Bonatti Pillar and numerous other incidents.

Climbing will always be dangerous but the best chance for survival is to serve a long apprenticeship slowly gaining experience and building your confidence to take the next step. It is these experiences that provide the data for the proper functioning of the intuitive process. An intuitive awareness of extreme situations is ultimately the most useful tool in the art of survival, even surviving one's own mistakes. On our second bivouac, 1000 metres up the North-East Spur of Les Droites, Adrian Burgess and I went to sleep on our narrow sloping ice ledges. I had a vivid dream where a friend was admonishing me for not attending to details, one of my faults. I woke and thought I had better check the knots of belays. I had tied them, but was shocked to find that I had forgotten to clip them into my harness. I could so easily have rolled off the ledge and back down to the glacier. Lose your dreams, lose your mind and maybe your life too.

(*above*) Bob Wark on Birthday Crack (Curbar) barracked by a ribald throng.

(*below*) The Brain on Curbar Edge in 1962. My dress included a patched Norwegian sweater and rather snazzy breeches made from my father's old police trousers – the truncheon holder was just right for my peg hammer. My first pair of PAs were given to me as a wedding present by Dennis Gray and Des Haldum, but after a year's heavy use were now showing distinct signs of distress. Until then I climbed everything in plimsolls.

(*above*) In 1976, with Americans Bill Westbay (*left*) and Doug Sniveley, on Alcasan (El), on the popular limestone cliffs at Stoney Middleton.

Nothing typifies the diversity of British rock climbing more than the adventurous ascents of sea stacks. The Old Man of Hoy is world-renowned but there are others, smaller but no less interesting. On a cold winter weekend in 1987 Jim Duff and I swam the Atlantic twice to climb The Old Man of Stoer and Am Buachaille in Sutherland, north-west Scotland. Am Buachaille (*right*) involves a two-pitch HVS climb which had added challenge in winter. An icy swim gave access to its plinth and we reached the summit with two long 4c pitches. We abseiled to regain the plinth and in the gathering gloom made a frightening return swim through the now turbulent tidal surges to complete a small but totally fulfilling expedition.

(*above*) Colin Downer at work during the
first winter ascent of Waterpipe Gully,
a 250m gutter choked with icicles.

(*left*) Paul Braithwaite leads the first pitch
of Hadrian's Wall on Ben Nevis and to its
right the celebrated Point Five Gully
stimulates all who seek to climb it – Guy
Lee on the second pitch (*below*).

In February 1986 my son Michael and I did the Direct Start to Route 2 and continued up Route 1 on the left side of Carn Dearg on Ben Nevis to complete an excellent iced-up rock climb (grade 4/5) of a type becoming increasingly popular.

SCOTTISH WINTER CLIMBING

These photographs reflect my years of winter climbing. I have done many of the classic gullies and ice faces and also some of the high mountain rock climbs in heavily iced conditions. Some of my best climbs have been away from the popular haunts – in Skye where during its rare freeze-ups, Jim Duff and I made the first winter ascent of The Smear (grade 5), and a few years later Colin Downer and I did the celebrated Waterpipe Gully. Frozen waterfall climbs are also entertaining, two of the more memorable being the Falls of Glomach in Kintail and Scales Force in the Lake District.

(*below left*) Ginger Cain, Jim Duff and Jane Wilson enjoying the ice canyon approach to the Falls of Glomach before our ascent in 1978. (*below right*) The Smear, Creag a'Mhadaidh, Skye which gave Jim Duff and me our hardest new route on ice.

ALPINE WINTER CLIMBING

During alpine seasons in the sixties I did a selection of Grandes Courses. After that expedition climbing took over and it was not until 1980 that I did my best alpine climb – a winter ascent of the North-East Spur of Les Droites, surely one of the finest mixed climbs in the Mont Blanc range. The route is impressively structured, with the first third up a wide rocky couloir and the upper part working a tenuous line up to the left of the great icy sweep of the North Face. I was partnered by Adrian Burgess, a very experienced alpine and expedition climber. Our bivouac on hacked out ice ledges high on the face with 1000m of steep rock and ice sweeping away below was particularly memorable.

Adrian Burgess on the North-East Spur of Les Droites: (*above*) in the initial couloir; (*right*) the first pitch out onto the North Face; (*near left*) typical climbing higher up; (*centre left*) the second bivouac site; (*far left*) on the ridge above the initial couloir with the North Face beyond.

2 Journeys to the Lands of Islam

1962–1967: Atlas, Tibesti, Cilo Dag and Hindu Kush

A Tibbu tribesman of the central Sahara. Many are armed, reflecting a warlike history when they enslaved negroes to the south and raided the Taureg of the Hoggar region. The French ended the Tibbu dominance and now the negroes run the country, leaving this once proud warrior race to sharpen their swords and spears and dream of the past.

By the time I was twenty I was married, with a flat and had a good job as a geography teacher. I was enjoying regular climbing in Britain and going to the Alps each summer. But the itch to explore as well as climb took me and my Nottingham friends to North Africa after our alpine season in 1962. One advantage of that area is that it was cheap and that was important where we had to do everything on a shoestring. But the chief attraction was the romance of travelling among the isolated people of a remote and rugged terrain that had been marched over by Hannibal and the Foreign Legion and immortalised in the writings of Wilfred Thesiger.

So in 1962, on half-paid leave, I set off with Ray Gillies, Clive Davies, Steve Read and Steve Bowes. After hitch-hiking through Spain, calling in on the Sierra Nevada en route, we crossed the Straits of Gibraltar and hitch-hiked to Marakesh, where an overladen bus took us up into the High Atlas. We declined the services of a local guide, despite his impressive letter of recommendation from Wilf Noyce, and set off into the heart of the mountains and did several excellent rock climbs and reached most of the main summits, including Toubkal, the highest point in North Africa. After this we walked south for eighty miles to the Anti Atlas climbing Volcan Siroua on the way. This was in Berber country where we enjoyed their legendary desert hospitality. Our own cooking – wild mushrooms in gravy powder over a burning sage bush – grew more experimental as we ran out of supplies.

Despite the modest nature of our climbing objectives, the chance to visit new and unusual country and to move as a self-contained unit among mountain peoples was enormously satisfying – and a pattern I was to repeat again and again on my expeditions. The six-week trip cost us just £22 per head.

Going to the Sahara was the natural extension of going to the Atlas, and two years later the objective for my first organised expedition was therefore to the Tibesti Mountains

(*above*) After crossing Libya we entered Chad by the Korizo Pass, travelling below the impressive sandstone towers of the Aiguilles de Sisse.

Four impoverished climbers looking towards the Atlas Mountains.

of northern Chad. We were given £400 by the Mount Everest Foundation and bought three army lorries, one of which we cannibalised for spares. Our first efforts at raising local sponsorship resulted, after seventy-five begging letters, in a contribution of 40lbs of dried dates from a local trader. Hardly the top of anyone's shopping list for going to the Sahara!

At the last oasis in Libya we filled our water tanks. For the next 400 miles there would be nothing. Geographically, however, the journey was rich, as we found clumps of fossilised wood and lacustrine deposits, indications of the Sahara's balmier pre-desert days. In the Mourzouk Sand Sea, where the hottest temperatures in the world are recorded, the differential on the back axle of one of the lorries collapsed. Ray Gillies, our motor mechanic, took eight hours to complete a heroic repair job, with sand swirling around in a cool winter temperature of just 115°F.

We had relegated our guide to the rear lorry when it became apparent he only knew the camel tracks, so it was more by luck than judgment we arrived at General Leclerc's road through the Korizo Pass, the gateway to Chad and the Tibesti. We drove below the 450m sandstone towers of the Aiguilles de Sisse and up to one of the most spectacular views of the whole trip along the rim of a huge volcanic crater known as the Trou au Natron. Over 600m deep and seven miles across, a DC3 is said

A critical point during our Sahara journey was when the differential on the back axle of one of our lorries collapsed under the strain of driving through soft sand. Ray Gillies and Pete Warrington worked for eight hours in withering heat to make the vital repair.

The Cilo Dag mountains of Eastern Turkey. The highest peak in the range is Resko Tebbe (4170m), the second main peak from the left in this view from the north-east. The area, though limestone, is reminiscent of the Bregaglia, and has several small glaciers.

to have once flown round inside the rim. In fading light we could just make out small sulphur cones sprouting out of the saltpan floor.

The Tibbu of this area were a warrior race who conquered the neighbouring people and took negro slaves. When the French arrived in Chad in the 1930s they subdued the Tibbu and freed the slaves. It was now the negroes who ran the bureaucracy of the Tibesti and inspected our visas before we set off for Tarso Tieroko, the unclimbed 3000m mountain which was the ostensible objective of our expedition. Tieroko is the highest point of another eroded crater rim, its North Face falling some 600–900m to the crater floor. Access is complicated by unmarked waddy gorges which carve up the terrain, and the only water comes from remote stagnant pools polluted by wild goats. Ray and I scrambled onto the West Ridge, and then traversed across the South-West Face to a shallow gully leading up for 75m. The smooth rock here was the best we had met and gave quite hard climbing. The next 75m needed some care: VS climbing up lumps of cinder that threatened to pull out of the sandy rock matrix. Afterwards an easy scramble led to the summit. The climb was over so quickly that on the following day we made two more first ascents, one from the south by Ray Gillies and Pete Warrington, and another from the north by Clive Davies and me.

We had laid plans to return to the Tibesti, but two years later the King of Libya was overthrown by Colonel Gadaffi who soon began a military adventure in Chad. With the area a war zone the mountains have remained closed to foreigners ever since, which is sad because it is a part of the world which has left an indelible impression on me. For the first time, but not the last, it made me consider the vast differences between the self-contained existence of these desert and mountain-dwellers, compared with our overcomplicated way of living 5000 miles away, and wonder who has got it right.

In 1966 I organised an expedition of twenty youth club lads and schoolboys to the mountains of Kurdistan. Our climbing in the Cilo Dag area was necessarily modest, but it was fascinating to live among the Kurds on the mountainous border of Turkey and Iraq which unfortunately became familiar in television news footage in the aftermath of the Gulf War. Even in those days they were having bloody skirmishes with Iraqi troops across the border.

The next year, 1967, twelve of us set

A friendly group of Kurdish nomads who visited our camp in the Cilo Dag.

In the Hindu Kush we used horses and mules for transport between the various mountain groups. The horses were particularly useful for crossing rivers swollen with afternoon melt water.

off to go even further east for something altogether more ambitious – Koh-i-Bandaka in the Central Hindu Kush. At 6843m (22,445ft) it would be our first taste of high-altitude mountaineering and we had everything to learn.

Ray Gillies and I, supported by Tony Watts and Guy Lee, went straight up the valley onto the glacier at 5500m and made the first ascent of the South Face of Bandaka with headaches and sickness all the way. We spent two nights on the face in snow caves, and crossed two rock steps, after the second of which we realised, not only were we on our last legs, but we were going to find it very difficult to descend by the way we had come. However, recognising that we were now committed to the summit, from which we could descend by the easier West Ridge, somehow gave us a renewed burst of energy as our down-thinking ditherings were channelled into an upward direction. It is the case with many climbs I have done when, once I've found myself totally committed, it has gone along much more easily than expected.

We reached the summit and headed off down the West Ridge in swirling mist. A short distance below the top Ray's crampon came off and, on steep green ice, his feet shot from under him and he was hurtling towards the glacier 2000m below. The rope ran through my fingers and I braced myself to be pulled off after him, but with only a few loops left in my hand, he slid straight into a rock and came to a shaken but living halt. It was an eventful end to our first big mountain climb. After this we moved to the unclimbed mountains above the Sharan Valley. Now acclimatised and fit, and in perfect weather, we climbed seven more peaks which offered a mix of excellent granite, fine ice couloirs and elegant snow ridges. This trip had all the aspects that make a satisfactory expedition because of the variety of climbing we were able to enjoy.

Looking back, I realise how lucky I was to be able to visit the Tibesti Mountains, the mountains of Kurdistan and the central Hindu Kush when I did, as politics have since closed all three areas to foreigners. I only hope the people who showed us such amazing hospitality and generosity of spirit have survived the turbulent events of recent years.

Free French oildrums mark the Korizo Pass.

Not much shade in the Sahara from the 120°F temperatures.

TIBESTI MOUNTAINS, CHAD, 1962

Our passage across the Sahara was as much a part of the adventure as the climbing in the Tibesti. We had everything to learn about desert travel. It was a fascinating journey of contrasts, from the daytime heat over the shimmering rock and gravel plain with the constant clanking of the sand tracks and the sickening smell of oil and petrol, to the evening camps with the sun setting in the desert haze through pink to purple in perfect silence.

One of our two lorries dwarfed by the huge Aiguilles de Sisse where we made a number of climbs.

Tarso Tieroko, some three days' walking beyond the isolated village of Modra.

Steve Bowes makes a friend in Yebbi Bou.

A Tibbu woman prepares food in Modra.

TIBESTI MOUNTAINS (continued)

In Chad we based ourselves in a rented hut in Modra at the head of the Modra Wadi. This was three days' march from the Tieroko mountains we hoped to climb. Despite their harsh conditions the villagers were a resourceful, fun-loving bunch, and almost completely self-sufficient. The date palm provided food, fuel, shelter and animal fodder. Its trunk fibres were used for saddle pads, rope and baskets. Goats provided occasional fresh meat and daily milk; their hair spun for clothing yarn and their skins used for dagger sheaths, gourds, saddles and harness. Only a few metal goods and fabrics were brought in from elsewhere.

(right) Clive Davies, Ray Gillies and Pete Warrington set off on the three-day march to Teiroko.

With a guide and three mules
we began our long and arid
approach march.

Apart from its 900m North Face,
Tieroko offered no great problems
and we made three new routes. The
main difficulties were the layers of
loose conglomerate near the
summit. The top provided
fine views of the fossilized river
systems of the area.

CILO DAG MOUNTAINS, TURKEY 1966

Most of our five-week school holiday expedition to Turkish Kurdistan was spent travelling with little time left for climbing. We saw enough to know this was an area worth returning to one day, with uncharted rock walls of up to 600m awaiting ascents. There are several small receding glaciers and winter climbing may well be a better option, for the rock is loose but highly featured; even in summer, cracks and crevices are choked with snow and ice.

Our most interesting climb was the first ascent of the elegant 200m spire of Cafer Kule (*right*) which I climbed with Brian Palmer.

(*below*) As we drove south-east from Lake Van into the heart of Kurdistan we passed below Hosab Castle.

(*above*) Sharan, a typical Afghan mountain village in the centre of the Hindu Kush. (*below*) Crossing the Kokcha river near the roadhead at the Sarisang mine.

HINDU KUSH, 1967

We used lorries again for an expedition to the higher peaks of the Hindu Kush in Afghanistan. At Kabul the twelve climbers split into two groups. Our northern group of Mick Terry, Ray Gillies, Ken Vickers, Guy Lee, Tony Watts and myself concentrated on the peaks above the Sakhi and Sharan valleys.

The local area has much in common with the valleys of the Atlas Mountains where a similar environment and culture gives rise to the same methods of house-building, field-terracing, irrigation, making sickles and building water mills for grinding corn.

The road passed Hazarati-i-Sayet and ended at the Lapis Lazuli mine at Sarisang from where we used mules and horses to progress.

(*above left*) A villager using an 1857 flintlock rifle. (*above right*) Members of the expedition (*l to r*) Doug Scott, Ken Vickers, Bill Cheverst, Brian Palmer, Mick Terry, Guy Lee; (*seated*) Bob Holmes, Ray Gillies, George Jones, Tony Watts, Dick Stroud and two hitch-hikers.

The local people made us welcome though we had to work hard to get good hire rates for the mules we needed to carry equipment up the mountain valleys. One muleteer stayed on to help shift loads to higher camps out of friendly curiosity. Later we hired horses to make a 200-mile journey (*below*) to the Panjshir Valley to join the southern group. Here we discovered that John Fleming had been tragically swept to his death in the Panjshir river.

Our main target was a new route up Koh-i-Bandaka but we made the mistake of moving straight up to tackle this without any acclimatisation and consequently suffered on the climb. After this we had a field day, climbing ten peaks in six weeks. We approached the mountains as if they were an extension of the Alps but despite our acclimatisation errors on Bandaka we were fit enough to take full advantage of the almost continuous good weather.

(*right*) The South Face of Koh-i-Bandaka. We climbed the couloir just right of the centre of the face and then descended the left-hand ridge.

(*below*) Guy Lee and I in the igloo we dug at the foot of the South Face after two intermediate camps.

Ray Gillies in action during the climb: (*below left*) at our first bivouac at 6400m; (*centre*) on the rocks of the first step; (*right*) with old Japanese flags on the summit; (*below right*) on the descent.

After our Koh-i-Bandaka ascent we moved to the peaks above the Sharan Valley where we made a number of enjoyable climbs on good rock and reliable ice. These pictures show Tony Watts in action during our ascent of the North-West Couloir of Berast Sharan (*inset*) and on the lower slopes of the East Face of Koh-i-Sisgeikh.

The view from Koh-i-Sisgeikh to Koh-i-Morusq (6435m). The nearer 5850m top was climbed by Guy Lee and Mick Terry on the same day.

HINDU KUSH (continued)

Now the Soviets have pulled out of Afghanistan we can look forward to the day when various factions sort out their rivalries so that this war-ravaged country can return to some sort of normality. Then the climbers may be allowed to return to rediscover this harsh yet hospitable land and continue the exploration of its marvellous mountains.

(*left*) The final ridge to the summit of Koh-i-Sisgeikh (6130m).

(*right*) The fine rock climbing on the East Face of Koh-i-Sisgeikh.

EVEREST: A TASTE OF THE BIG TIME

A telephoto of the South-West Face of Everest, encrusted with late monsoon snow. With its base at 8000m, the Rock Band bars access to the upper face.

3 Everest: A Taste of the Big Time

Three expeditions to Everest's South-West Face

It was Don Whillans who asked me if I fancied going to Everest for a spring 1972 attempt on the unclimbed South-West Face. The only snag was the expedition was being led by Dr Karl Herrligkoffer, infamous for his wrangles with the likes of Buhl and Messner. 'You can leave the doctor to me,' said Don. 'I can handle him.' And I had no doubt that Don could do just that.

Don was renowned as the hard man of British climbing; not only for his climbs, as he was reputed to be able to take on anyone. Legends about him were legion and I was always in awe of him: a little man but incredibly powerful. Once he came to Nottingham to lecture. He arrived five minutes before the start, gave the projectionist his slides, walked up onto the stage, stood in front of some 800 people and said, 'I'm Don Whillans. They say I'm working class but I'd like you to know I've not worked for twelve years.' His slides were awful but he had the audience in hysterics with his sharp wit and immaculate timing.

Don's invitation was a turning point in my climbing career. I'd never thought much of climbing Everest. This expedition was an Austro-German affair with a sprinkling of other nationalities with a total strength of eighteen. The British contingent consisted of Don, Hamish MacInnes and me. One might have thought Herrligkoffer wanted Don along for his experience in getting to 8380m on the face the previous year, but he was more interested in our fund-raising potential. He disliked me as a hippy totally superfluous to his requirements.

At the start of the expedition we had to make the route through the Ice-fall, one of the most lethal areas on the south side of the mountain, but especially beautiful in the mornings when the sun first catches the chaotic ice blocks and séracs. I found some of the Austrian climbers good mountain companions, and both then and later had a good relationship with many of them, but in 1972 one was always aware of simmering animosities, particularly towards Don as a result of his struggles with the European climbers on the International Expedition of the previous year.

Don, Hamish and I spent over two weeks on the face, establishing Camps 4 and 5 on slopes that were very rocky and clear of snow on this trip. We began by erecting the ingenious aluminium tent platforms Hamish had designed for the expedition. I acclimatised well but I still had a lot to learn from Don about saving energy. One day, feeling good, I rushed up to Camp 5 and started digging for loot in an old 1971 campsite. But as I sat down to rest, I realised I had done

Leaders of the big expeditions: Dr Karl Herrligkoffer (*above*) and Chris Bonington (*below* conferring with his 1975 Equipment Manager, Dave Clarke). Their styles differed. Chris was always closely involved with the action, whereas Dr Herrligkoffer conducted proceedings from Base Camp and was therefore divorced from the realities on the face.

The two Bonington expeditions were also properly financed, and well supported by specialist companies, so we had enough up-to-date equipment and clothing for both the climbers and sherpas – a key factor in our success.

too much. I was getting double vision. 'You've got to stop rushing about up here,' Don said. 'Take it easy. Come on, we'd better get off down.'

It was an interesting experience sharing a tent with Don. He wasn't one for camp chores and spent most of his time sleeping or thinking or adapting equipment. Above Base Camp I had cooked all the meals. I never minded that as I quite enjoyed cooking. But after a big solo effort to Camp 5 I came down the ropes yelling 'Get a brew on,' to find Don still tinkering with his equipment and no brew. I gathered snow, melted it down, got a brew on, passed it round, and then prepared the evening meal – mashed potatoes, sausage and peas – and handed that to Don. I said, 'I'm not your mother you know, Don.' He said, 'Oh, are you one of those people who moans about a bit of cooking?' He was so outrageous I had to smile.

Meanwhile the equipment needed for this siege climbing was simply not getting up the face and it seemed unlikely we would get any higher than Don's point of the year before. Morale had sunk very low so we descended and a few days later the expedition came to an end, defeated by cold and inadequate logistics.

Despite everything, it had been a fantastic experience for me to enter the legendary Western Cwm and go high on Everest. I had really enjoyed being with Hamish and Don, and with men like Horst Schneider, Adi Weissensteiner and Peter Perner, and I certainly enjoyed being on Everest. I found that I could take to altitude. I had used oxygen on some days, other days I hadn't, and it didn't seem to make a lot of difference once I had acclimatised.

I was to get my second chance to tackle the South-West Face sooner than I'd expected. Chris Bonington had permission for that autumn and asked Hamish and me along. But he did not invite Don. Knowing what a crushing blow this would be for him, Hamish and I pressed Don's case. After all, no one knew the South-West Face better than he. But Chris was adamant that he could not function as leader with Don on the expedition. So we were back in the Western Cwm with our leader throwing one team after another at the South-West Face, tilting at that great windmill in the sky, but all his efforts and ours came to naught. It was too late in the year to be climbing steep rock above 8000m. On November 14 I stood at the high point with Dougal Haston and Mick Burke, looking up at a vertical corner maybe 250m high, screaming into each other's

ears to be heard above the wind roaring across the upper reaches. Dougal had already decided – I only concurred – we'd better get down.

On the descent I studied a gully on the left side of the face. It seemed like there might be a way through the Rock Band there. Something I've never really understood was why two experienced climbers like Dougal and Don could have spent so much time around that right-hand gully in 1971 and 1972 when this hidden gully offered a far more logical and committing line.

Chris got his second chance in 1975 by which time I had gathered a lot more high-altitude experience and become accustomed to sponsored expeditions and Chris's leadership style, although I could never accept it totally. In fact the 1975 expedition was a very happy one, the left-hand gully indeed

Hamish MacInnes, Don Whillans and me at Advance Base Camp in May, 1972 wearing our special down suits and rubber overboots that Don had developed for the 1970 Annapurna and 1971 Everest expeditions. This clothing was a major asset compared to the heavier traditional alpine clothing (including enormous triple boots) adopted by most of the other team members (see photo on page 36).

Mick Burke, who disappeared near the summit of Everest in 1975. Mick, a fine alpinist, had played major roles on Annapurna (1970) and Everest (1972). After this he concentrated on a career as a TV cameraman, in which capacity he came to Everest in 1975. Despite a long lay off he was still strong enough to make a solo summit bid. Sadly, a sudden storm foiled what would have been an outstanding individual effort.

proved to be the key to the Rock Band, and we were successful where so many others, including ourselves, had previously failed. Dougal Haston and I reached the summit on September 24 in the course of a remarkable three days spent above 8000m. The fact that on our descent we had to bivouac just below the summit at 8760m without oxygen gave me a lot of confidence for the future. If I could survive a night up there without oxygen and a sleeping bag, and avoid frostbite, I could probably survive a night out anywhere where there was snow to dig into to escape the biting winds. The climb was repeated the following day by Pete Boardman and Pertemba, closely followed by Mick Burke, climbing solo. But elation turned to despair when a storm hit the summit area and Mick failed to return. As we waited we became more and more subdued until it was clear that Mick, with his pugnacious yet warm-hearted personality, wouldn't be around to challenge our pretentions any more. It was a sobering reminder of how a sudden change in the weather can bring disaster on Everest.

The one thing that this expedition surely demonstrated was that if a project is well organised with enough experienced climbers and ample Sherpa support, then success can more or less be guaranteed on anything, providing the weather is reasonable. But having proved this fact, what is the point of repeating the exercise? Climbing is all about facing the unknown and the outcome should remain uncertain until the end. Climbers who seek to push back the frontiers will always wish to tackle Everest and other big mountains in an adventurous way. That means going more lightweight, without continuous lines of fixed ropes between fixed camps, which is only possible without bottled oxygen. The line that has to be rigged to allow these supplies to be ferried up the mountain also becomes a safety rope that allows rapid retreat in the event of any difficulties or discomforts, bad weather or illness. It is only when climbers part company with the fixed ropes that proper climbing begins.

On the final few hundred yards to the summit of Everest, breaking trail through crusty snow, my thoughts seemed to separate from the body and gave direction from a position centred over my left shoulder. When I was going too fast, and stumbling knee-deep through the crust, my mind would suggest to my body that it had better slow down and get the rhythm going again or I wouldn't make it. Then when I was veering too far to the right, my mind, looking down on the process, would give a warning that if I kept going in that direction I would probably fall through a cornice and plummet down the Kangshung Face. These out of body experiences are often reported by high-altitude climbers. It does seem that in those circumstances, pushing yourself to the limit, and with limited oxygen, food and water intake, the climber is able to tap hidden reserves to keep him alive – not just reserves of energy but also levels more profound.

I learnt a lot from my three siege-style expeditions to Everest South-West Face. I shall always be grateful to Don and then Chris for the opportunities and it was on Everest that I forged an all-to-brief, but in every way satisfactory climbing partnership with Dougal. It also gave me the confidence to start planning a trip to Kangchenjunga but I knew that it would be a lightweight venture, with a small team and definitely no bottles of oxygen.

(*left*) A laddered section in the Khumbu Ice-fall. (*right*) Adi Huber, Leo Breitenberger, Felix Kuen and Werner Haim who we dubbed the Big Four since they occupied the lead as long as possible, despite growing fatigue.

EVEREST, SOUTH-WEST FACE, 1972

My first experience of Everest was load-carrying up the shifting Khumbu Ice-fall and the Western Cwm, supporting the Big Four lead climbers of the Herrligkoffer expedition. The route was advanced at a funereal pace and eventually we set up the Whillans Boxes at Camp 4 and pressed on to Camp 5. Unfortunately, a group of the climbers became convinced that Don Whillans was hogging the lead. These animosities, combined with a poor flow of supplies and weak leadership, brought about the expedition's failure.

Carrying sections of platform framework up to the site of Camp 4. The remains of earlier camp platforms can be seen above. The inset photo shows the Whillans Boxes erected on MacInnes platforms.

EVEREST, 1972 AND 1975

The British South-West Face
expeditions of 1972 and 1975 took
place in the autumn when the face is
plastered with monsoon snow and ice.
This is steadily swept and scoured by
blustery winds as winter approaches.
These conditions produced a whole
new set of problems and hampered
logistical support. The main technical
problem was to find a way through
the huge Rock Band that bars the way
to the upper face. All the attempts
before 1975 looked for a route at its
right-hand end but in 1975 we went
straight for the gully on the left and
found that it contained sufficient snow
to provide a way through.

(*left and above*) At the foot of the gully and quitting it for the ramp higher up.

EVEREST, SOUTH-WEST FACE, 1975

Nick Estcourt and Paul Braithwaite climbed the gully in fine style in a single day, first using the gully bed and then taking a snow-covered ramp leading up to the right. The gully had been recently swept by avalanches so snow conditions were good. Above this Dougal Haston and I, supported by Ang Phurba, Chris Bonington, Mike Thompson, Mick Burke and Lhakpa Dorje, established and stocked Camp 6 at 8300m as the base for the summit bid.

(*below*) Looking up to the ramp from the gully

Dougal Haston clears a platform for Camp 6   The upper part of the face – we traversed the lower snow slopes and climbed the couloir on the right.

Dougal sets off from Camp 6 heading for the break in the first band of rocks to gain the upper snow slopes which led across to the South Summit Couloir.

Approaching the South Summit Couloir.

Moving up snow slopes above the rock step in the couloir with Western Cwm far below.

Using telephoto lenses, the other members of the expedition photographed our progress across the upper slopes.

EVEREST, 1975 (continued)

After a day of fixing ropes we set off on the summit bid at dawn, reaching the South Summit Couloir by 1 p.m. Here we overcame a 20m rock pitch up the soft Yellow Band and forced a way up unconsolidated snow in the couloir to gain the South Summit at 3 p.m. We suspected that the summit ridge might also be unstable, so we rested and considered our next move. One possibility was to bivouac where we were and continue in the morning but, knowing how wretched I feel after a bivouac, I was keen to avoid this. After a rest and a brew I led a pitch along the ridge and found that the snow was more consolidated.

(*left*) Brewing up on the saddle by the South Summit (8760m) at the point where we would bivouac on our descent. The summit ridge is in the background.

EVEREST, 1975 (continued)

The Hillary Step, normally a rock pitch, was banked out in monsoon snow with a granular quality, like sugar, that demanded the greatest care. The photomontage above is made up from the last two pictures of the film. But as I was putting the camera away, I found a roll of high-speed Ektachrome, exactly what was required with night approaching. We continued up the corniced ridge which opened onto the summit and as the shadows lengthened we reached the top. The view in the low light of sunset was astounding and we gazed in all directions, taking pictures and soaking up a unique experience. After an hour we descended to face our night of frigid bivouacking at the South Summit.

(*left*) On the ridge before the Hillary Step.

Slow going in deep snow up the final summit slopes.

My Everest summit photo.

Dougal in front of the setting sun with the head of Rongbuk Glacier below on the right, Cho Oyu beyond and Shishapangma on the far horizon.

4 Big Wall Climbing

Cima Ovest, El Capitan, the Troll Wall and Mount Asgard

Rock climbing is, for me, the most enjoyable part of mountaineering. Between visits to far flung corners of Africa and Asia I spent most weekends on cliffs in Britain, and on holidays in the Alps and Dolomites I did many alpine rock climbs. This gradually pushed up my standard, although it was never anywhere near the highest of the day.

In addition to my normal rock climbing, by the mid-1960s I had got heavily involved in artificial climbing. In Britain pegging, as it was called, began in quarries and on under-exploited limestone cliffs. From 1950 to the mid-60s peggers had a field day, enjoying a relatively safe, strenuous and yet wild climbing experience on steep cliffs, the more overhanging the better. It was especially stimulating when the wind, rain or snow were lashing around the crags and you could stay dry, steadily progressing across the overhanging rock.

All this limestone pegging contributed to growing success in the Alps and the big routes on the Dru and the Grand Capucin and many of the major Dolomite climbs were soon ascended regularly by British climbers who had mastered the artificial skills. With the newly formed Nottingham Climbers' Club I did many aid routes during the winter weekends on the limestone overhangs of High Tor, Malham or Gordale, and this later gave me the confidence to climb routes like the Yellow Edge and the Comici in the Tre Cime and the West Face of the Aiguille du Blaitière and the Bonatti Pillar in the Mont Blanc group.

By 1968 this interest had developed into a curious and somewhat quirky obsession to climb underneath major overhangs. When I look back on those ventures I can still feel the tension mounting – I was fascinated by the challenge of overcoming the fear of hanging, bat-like, under roofs all day, in some cases day after day. The biggest overhang I found in England and Wales was a thirty metre monstrosity at North Stack, Anglesey, which Brian Palmer and I steadily wrestled into submission during three wet and snowy December weekends. When I heard about the huge overhanging face or Nose of Strone Ulladale, in Harris (Outer Hebrides) I was determined to get up there and make the first ascent. It took Guy Lee, Mick Terry, Jeff Upton and me three days to climb it in 1969 and in later years, on the same cliff I added Sidewinder with Guy Lee, and the most difficult of all our aid climbs in Britain, the Nose Direct, on which Guy and I were joined by the leading American big wall climber, Dennis Hennek.

The biggest roof climb I could find anywhere was the North Face Direct (Bauer/Rudolf route) on the Cima Ovest, which I climbed with Jeff Upton and Ted Wells in 1969. It had been repeated one or two times before and we were keen to make the first British ascent. Unknown to us Leo Dickinson, Brian Molyneaux and Jeff Morgan had got wind of our plans and tried to beat us to it. The lower section we mostly free climbed, marvelling at the paucity of pegs and the free-climbing ability of the early ascensionists. I even took a twenty metre fall when a loose peg pulled. After four or five pitches, we came to an abseil point and on the yellow limestone was scratched 'F... off Scott, it's too loose for you !' Leo's team had reached this point and then abseiled down, stripping some of the pegs on their descent. This challenge, of course, fired us with new determination and we passed on up to the roof. There I set off across the forty-five metre overhang. But it was so long that three-quarters of the way out I had exhaustion cramp knotting my fingers and creeping down my arms into my back. I didn't think I had the strength to return to the back wall. It was a case of having to go to the lip to get up the easier headwall beyond. When I realised there was no turning back and that I was fully committed, the last part of the route went much more easily.

The following year, 1970, I went over to the Mecca of big wall climbing, Yosemite Valley, California, where I teamed up with the Austrian guide, Peter Habeler, climbing first the Leaning Tower and then setting off to attempt the Salathé Wall of El Capitan. At that time all the major routes on El Capitan were held in awe by climbers throughout the world, including eastern-based American climbers. Mick Burke and Rob Wood had made the first non-American ascent of the Nose in 1968 and the Salathé, together with the North America Wall were seen as the next obvious targets. The Salathé certainly had Peter and me overawed, looking up from the El Cap meadow at those thirty-eight long and difficult pitches we had to climb.

At first Peter and I didn't get along too well. I think both of us were projecting our fears of this huge crag onto each other and we were easily niggled. I was very unhappy when I found that he had put salt tablets in our water supply and he was tetchy because I was much slower than he. He would call, 'Come, Doug – to rest is not to conquer.' This got me going as it was always accompanied by an offer to lead the offending pitch. *His* main problem, being only some five feet two inches tall, was in hauling the sack, the third man as we called it. However by the time we got to the overhang below the headwall all these problems had

Brian Palmer on the Big Overhang, Anglesey. This major aid climb took us three weekends to complete but, with much gear in place, it can now be done more quickly and has been soloed. A three-star A3, it is now an obvious target for free climbers.

Peter Habeler with haul bag (our third man) before our Salathé Wall ascent. A superb all-round climber, he later made innovative Himalayan ascents on Gasherbrum and Everest with Reinhold Messner – the latter being the first time the world's highest peak was climbed without bottled oxygen.

Rick White, the tough Brisbane climber with whom I teamed up to climb the Nose of El Capitan. Rick later took part in our ascent of the East Pillar of Shivling in 1981.

The enormous scale of the Nose of El Capitan is shown in this telephoto of climbers in the Boot Flake area halfway up the route (see also page 53).

sorted themselves, we had come together in harmony and our steady progress up those magnificent upper pitches was a delight.

It had been a fantastic five days on a vertical desert of rock. I had become so attuned to being there, I felt I could go on day after day and nothing else mattered. The weather was good, the rock was good and Peter proved a superb climbing companion. I remember walking over the dome of El Capitan with a heightening of sensory perception, presumably brought about by our ascetic goings-on down below for such an extended period. My sense of hearing was acute to the crackling pine cones under foot and my sense of smell caught the fragrance of the pines, while I was seeing greens inside greens inside the forest. The whole landscape became more vibrant and stayed that way quite a few days afterwards, as did the inner calm I was experiencing.

The next time I climbed El Capitan was in 1973. On that occasion I teamed up with the Australian, Rick White, to tackle the Nose. We hoped to make an ascent with as much free climbing as possible and, where aid was needed, use nuts and try to avoid peg bashing. The climb took four days and we largely succeeded in our objective. We only used fifteen in-situ pegs and the various existing bolt ladders, and managed to do more than sixty per cent of the climb free, though this added about a day to the ascent. For the most part it was perfect crack climbing, just the sort we both enjoyed, Rick with his Frog Buttress background and I from countless weekends on gritstone. It seemed to me that it was an even better rock climb than the Salathé Wall, mainly because there was more free climbing and because of its wonderful line at the apex of the two great granite faces of El Capitan.

Europe's answer to the Yosemite Valley is the Romsdal area of Norway. Here, in 1970, with my Nottingham friends, Ted Wells, Jeff Upton and Guy Lee, I climbed the celebrated Troll Wall. We made very fast time completing the 1500m face in a total of seventeen hours climbing spread over two days, halving the previous best time. On the same trip, with Terry Bolger, I also made the third ascent of Hoibakk's Chimney in heavy rain.

In the summer of 1971 I resigned my job as a school teacher. I had come to the end of the line when it came to getting leave of absence.

The logical extension of this big wall climbing, as Yvon Chouinard has pointed out, is to move on to the more remote ranges. For me that meant Baffin Island, Canada, an area of huge granite walls, the obvious place to apply big wall skills. On the first trip we got a good idea of the potential and I subsequently visited this region four times. I fell in love with the island, not just for its obvious climbing potential but also to walk those tundra valleys bathed in the spectral blue light of the north. The trip I enjoyed most was in 1972 when Paul Braithwaite, Paul Nunn and Dennis Hennek and I made a new 1400m route on the east side of Mount Asgard. This involved thirty-five hours of continuous climbing up forty-five hard and significant pitches. This was possible in the perpetual daylight up there on the Arctic Circle. We were sixty-five miles from the nearest Inuit (or Eskimo) settlement and there were no other climbers in the area. Had anything happened to any one of us the rest of the team would have had to sort out the problem. Climbing is about taking responsibility for your own lives and doing it in remote places like Baffin Island adds an extra dimension missing in more populated areas like the Alps or the Yosemite Valley. This is why our Mount Asgard climb remains one of the most satisfying big walls I have ever done.

(*above*) The 200m overhanging face of Strone Ulladale in the Outer Hebrides where we established three hard aid routes – the Scoop, Sidewinder and the Nose.

(*far left*) On the first pitch of the Scoop in 1969. The route has become popular but unfortunately bolts have been added. In 1990 Paul Pritchard and Johnny Dawes used it as the basis for a magnificent free route – surely one of the most challenging climbs in Britain?

(*near left*) With Guy Lee and Dennis Hennek before our 1971 ascent of the Nose – at A5 (sans bolts), our hardest Strone climb.

(*right*) On the North Face of Cima Ovest – swinging out under the 45m roof, 250m above the scres.

Jeff Upton on one of the initial pitches of the Troll Wall.

TROLL WALL, NORWAY, 1970

The 1200m Troll Wall (*right*) is highest rock face in Europe. It was first climbed by Tony Howard, Bill Tweedale and John Amatt in 1965 and, though harder and longer lines have been added since, their Rimmon Route (named after their club) remains the most popular way up the Troll Wall. The Romsdal Valley (*inset*) is full of rock walls, notably on the north faces of Sondre Trolltind and Trollryggen (the two peaks in the centre).

(*left*) During our methodical ascent of the Bauer/Rudolf roof of the Cima Ovest we had this fine view across to the easier and less steep (though more classic) Swiss/Italian route – an aid climb tailor-made for the attentions of the modern free climber. This Yugoslav climber is not soloing, his partner is belayed in a hidden niche just to his left.

Peter Habeler in action on the Salathé Wall: (*above left*) Climbing the Hollow Flake – the inner flake is no longer there; (*above right*) Belaying below the headwall and leading one of its overhanging pitches – the most spectacular part of the route.

SALATHÉ WALL, YOSEMITE, 1970

El Capitan is one of the biggest granite monoliths in the world, rising over 1000m from the Yosemite Valley with a scale that seems exaggerated by the smooth granite walls so as to become almost too huge to comprehend. It is daunting to pick out the thirty-eight

significant pitches that climbing the Salathé Wall or the Nose entails. The only way to cope is to select a feature for the day and aim for that, so that by nibbling away at the problem it eventually solves itself.

Among many fine climbers I met in Yosemite was Royal Robbins whose precision and enthusiasm were always

evident when we climbed together. It was thus good to make an ascent of his (and others') Salathé Wall with the Austrian guide Peter Habeler at the end of my first visit.

(*right*) El Capitan. The Nose generally follows the sunlit crest and the Salathé Wall takes a diagonal line up the shadowy walls on the left ending near the skyline step

The tension traverse to the Sickle Ledge. The route works up to the edge on the right and finishes up the obvious right-hand dihedral system.

THE NOSE, EL CAPITAN, 1973

I teamed up with the Australian Rick White to climb the Nose. We tried to climb free wherever possible and where aid was unavoidable use nuts/chocks rather than start pounding pegs. We were largely successful and thus I found the Nose an even more satisfying climb than Salathé Wall. Rick was totally unfazed on one of his first Yosemite climbs, despite the cold conditions of April.

(*left*) The wild running pendulum of the King Swing where the climber has to jump the chimney and try to reach the Stoveleg Cracks.

Rick White on the bolt ladder that crosses the blank rock between the Texas and Boot Flakes and (*below left*) moving up beyond the Great Roof.

(*above*) A typical Baffin mountain scene of valley, cliff and glacier. The rock pillar of Breidablik (*centre*) provided a fine climb for Phil Koch and Guy Lee that was later repeated by Dennis Hennek, Rob Wood and myself.

BAFFIN ISLAND 1971

Our experiences in Yosemite had left a number of us with a desire to apply our big wall skills further afield. Rob Wood and I therefore organised a trip to investigate the big walls of Baffin Island. It was an Anglo-American group with Yosemite experts Dennis Hennek and Phil Koch, my Nottingham friends Ray Gillies, Steve Smith and Guy Lee, and Rob Wood and Mick Burke who had climbed El Cap's Nose route together in 1968. The final member was the veteran Baffin expert, Pat Baird who had led the 1953 trip that made many first ascents. We flew to Frobisher Bay which was being developed with amenities for the Inuit, and continued to Pangnirtung.

(*left*) Members of the 1971 party: (*l to r*) Steve Smith, Ray Gillies, Dennis Hennek, Guy Lee, Phil Koch, myself and Rob Wood.

Inuit mothers contemplate the facilities of Frobisher Bay.

The Inuit had not adapted to the 'benefits' of civilisation, the result being a major increase in TB, VD, alcoholism and the suicide rate. By 1976 there was a move back to the summer camping grounds and attempts to market Inuit carvings. The Inuit have much in common with the Sherpas. Both live in extreme environments and still have the intuitive processes that has ensured their survival. Their future is now very much at the mercy of change.

An Inuit girl who later died of TB.

Inuit boys making a meal out of raw seal meat at Pangnirtung.

(*below left*) Approached up Pangnirtung Fjord using boats and skidoos. (*below right*) A typical Baffin camp below Mount Turnweather.

(*above*) Mount Asgard from the south-east. Guy Lee, Phil Koch and Rob Wood climbed the South Buttress of South Peak (left) in 1971. The original route to the North Peak goes up from the central col and the East Pillar is on the right.

(*left*) A view along the West Face with the South Buttress on the right. Charlie Porter's climb to North Peak started below the middle snow patch.

(*below*) Dennis Hennek on the lower slabs of the East Pillar with the chimneys of the final tower high above.

(*above*) In dull light at 2 a.m. Hennek leads the crux chimney of the East Pillar.

BAFFIN ISLAND, 1972

Dennis Hennek and I returned with Paul Braithwaite and Paul Nunn to try the West Face of Mount Asgard, but we soon ran into blank rock and had to withdraw, as we carried no bolts on this or any of our Baffin trips. We moved to the East Face and in thirty-five hours continuous climbing did a wonderful free route, generally about 5.7 but with some pitches of 5.8 (including a brutish chimney). We had a nightmare descent on soft snow, but this couldn't dampen our elation after such a fine route.

(*right*) On the descent we passed the 600m prow of Mount Friga's West Pillar.

5 *Short Trips to Far Away Places*

1974: Changabang and Pik Lenin   1976: Denali and Mount Kenya
1978 and 1985: Mount Waddington and Mount Colonel Foster

(*above*) The Canadian wilderness experience – Rob and Laurie Wood and Janine Caldbeck struggle up the steep forest slopes of the Homathko Valley during our approach to Mount Waddington in May, 1978.

Although Everest dominated my attentions in the early seventies, I managed before and after 1975 to get in some interesting and varied expeditions.

The mountains of the Garhwal had been closed to foreigners more or less since the British left India. In 1974, Chris Bonington managed to persuade the Indian authorities to permit an Indo-British expedition to Changabang, on the rim of the Nanda Devi Sanctuary. This was the unclimbed shark's tooth of shining granite that has fascinated climbers from Longstaff onwards.

Martin Boysen and Dougal Haston were the other British climbers in our team of four and the Indian group were the urbane Colonel Balwant Sandhu, the overall leader of the expedition, Kiran Kumar, Ujagar Singh and D. J. Singh.

We approached from the Rhamani Glacier and then crossed the difficult Shipton's Col to get to the South Face. We climbed this and then the East Ridge. All four Britons, Balwant Sandhu and Sherpa Tashi Chewang gained the top in a two-day push.

The other Sherpa on the trip was our cook, Norbu. He had been on Kangchenjunga in 1928 and Everest in 1936. The climber who had impressed him most was Bill Tilman for his unflagging energy and leadership qualities. Norbu laughed at our lavishly equipped kitchen, compared with Tilman's notorious austerity. But he admired our efforts on the mountain, disappearing for five days, carrying all our own food and gear up very hard steep terrain.

Almost immediately after Changabang I set off again for the Pamirs. Compared with the dramatic challenge of Changabang, these humpy mountains have little to offer the alpinist, with rotten snow, crumbling rock and the occasional earth tremor to start it all moving downhill.

The Russians had turned the Pamirs into a highly organised climbing area. On the meet we attended there were contingents from twenty countries including Estonians in their huge clinkered boots, a strong American team, French, Austrians, Scots and Japanese. To cater for all this activity a permanent Base Camp is equipped with hot food and showers.

'Send us your leader to haul up your flag at the opening ceremony' was the first thing we were asked on arrival. That really stopped us in our tracks. We explained that we had no leader or a flag and had no time for nationalistic ceremonies at mountaineering events. The problem was solved when a member of the Scottish contingent remembered that it was his flag too and hauled it up alongside the others.

We hoped to attempt a new line on the South-East Face of Pik Lenin (7135m/ 23,406ft) and approached this over the 5790m Krylenko Pass. Eventually excessive soft snow and illness in the team drove us back and we were lucky to escape the avalanches that engulfed other parties. After a rest we ascended Pik Lenin by the safest looking route, a previously unclimbed line up a snow and ice spur leading up from the north-east.

The day after our arrival back at Base we heard the radio calls from a Russian women's team high on Pik Lenin whose tents had blown away and whose members were slowly dying of exposure. We joined the French and Russian rescue party but when rescuers reached the scene they found that there were no survivors from a team of eight. When we got back to Base the closing celebrations were already under way with visiting dignitaries in attendance. Slowly it dawned on us that the helicopters that would have speeded our rescue attempts had been held to ship in these worthies. It left an unpleasant taste.

After our ascent of Everest both Dougal and I made lecture tours to North America so we arranged to meet and go to Alaska to attempt a new route (suggested to us by Bradford Washburn) up the South Face of Mount McKinley or Denali as it is called these days.

It was good to be back among the mountains of the north and good to be just a two-man team on a big mountain, especially one as challenging as Denali. We reached the foot of the face using skis and snow shoes and ensconced ourselves in an old igloo to prepare for the climb. Once we set off up our 50° ice route with its light covering of snow we gradually became aware of the enormous scale of our undertaking. We made good progress on the first day, despite being

Balwant Sandhu, leader of the 1974 Indo-British Changabang expedition and a later joint trip to Shivling. Shrewd and diplomatic, he was keenly aware that Indian climbers had much to learn about technical climbing and supported joint trips to achieve this.

We lost the path through the dense and dangerous forest approach to Kilimanjaro – Paul Braithwaite is alert for a possible leopard attack.

Paul on the lower Breach Wall of Kilimanjaro. The rotten ice gave no purchase for Terrordactyls and our ropes were badly cut by rockfall.

engulfed in a huge snow slough, and just before dark reached a suitable bivouac ledge. One night turned into two as a storm blew in and continued into the third day. It was early that morning I said to Dougal, 'Well, what do you reckon?' My sleeping bag was already wet and far too thin for the freezing cold temperatures. The hard Scotsman looked at me and said, 'You havnae got frostbite yet, have you?' Ah, I thought and answered, 'No, not even frostnip.' 'Well then,' he shrugged. Enough said, I thought, so we go on until we get frostbite and hope we get to the summit before that happens, which was the case, but only just, for we had altogether four nights out in the open and three in snow caves, including one below the summit. We had experienced hurricane-force winds and constant sub-zero temperatures. By the time we reached that final bivvy we were both feeling the effects of altitude which seems to be more acute at these latitudes – more like being at 7000m than 6000.

On the seventh day we walked over the summit and began our descent. Quite soon we encountered two young climbers sitting in the snow in a stupor and very badly frostbitten. They asked us to go down to the rest of their party so that they might radio to the Park Service to send up a helicopter. We made them as comfortable as we could and hastened down and eventually found four of their friends below the Denali Pass at 5200m. They had no means of contacting the Park Service and while two of them went up to be with the stricken climbers, we went on down to raise help. There was no helicopter available that could manage to fly up to 5800m, so we all had to go back up to bring them down lower. Eventually the helicopter came and whisked them off to Anchorage Hospital but nothing could be done to save them from having most of their hands and feet amputated. They were only in their early twenties. It was a real tragedy.

Just like the authorities in the Pamirs, the Denali Park Service at that time put great reliance on radio contact as a means of saving life in an emergency. But these radios not only lull climbers into a false sense of security, but when an actual crisis develops a rescue is often difficult or impossible. On these big mountains, indeed on any mountains, the emphasis should always be on individual responsibility.

After Denali I joined up with Paul Braithwaite to climb on Mount Kenya and Kilimanjaro. The exotic vegetation and rapid changes from tropical jungle to alpine grasslands opened up a new world to us. Our chief objective was the East Face of Mount Kenya by a new route generously pointed out to us by the local experts, Iain Allan and Ian Howell, who had been trying it themselves. It proved to be one of the best rock climbs on the mountain, with climbing averaging 5a/5.8 but with some taxing 5c/5.10 sections at 4900m. The route finished on the summit of Nelion. We also climbed the wonderful ice route up the Diamond Couloir and sampled more ice on Kilimanjaro.

Kilimanjaro is an amazing mountain, with cliffs of ice, like bergs, on top of dry cinder ash. On the approach we promptly lost our way in the dense, leopard-infested jungles on the lower slopes. Never before had I felt so pleased to find litter on a mountain, as it confirmed we were on course. We attempted a direct start to the Breach Wall, but after three pitches retired under a bombardment of friable rock and atrociously melting ice, and prudently opted for the Umbwe route to gain the surrealistic summit.

Rob Wood had emigrated to Canada, had married and was now building an alternative life style from a base on Vancouver Island. After our Baffin Island

trip of 1971 he had become deeply committed to Canadian-style pioneer mountaineering and in the early spring of 1978 invited me to join him and others to tackle the celebrated Mount Waddington, highest point in British Columbia. I jumped at the chance to visit such a mountain, famed for its associations with the likes of the Mundays, Wiessner and House. Apart from being very difficult, this fine peak is particularly inaccessible, being guarded by trackless forest terrain, the epitome of the Canadian wilderness experience. Although Waddington is only 4017m/13,177ft high we had to trek in through dense forests from sea level to a Base Camp at only 1300m.

The East Face of Mount Colonel Foster on Vancouver Island. We climbed the gully falling to the left from the highest point which provided a multi-pitched ice route (*below*).

This left 2700m of snow and ice climbing all of it remote from any possibility of help.

Five of us headed up the South-East Ridge which was very arduous in its deep covering of soft snow with many cornices. After a cold bivouac on the ridge, we established a spacious and secure bivouac site in a bergschrund below the difficult summit rock towers that had caused so many problems for the early pioneers. Eventually Rob and I pressed on to tackle the final tower. The South-East Couloir was still caked in winter snow but we made steady progress up the final chimneys and ice-plastered cracks. It was hard cramponing and exhausting in winter gear climbing over chockstones, under chockstones and out onto the surrounding walls. But as the day was ending we could see the summit and before long we had achieved the realisation of Rob's private dream which had brought us all to this lonely and wondrous mountain range.

In 1985 Greg Child and I joined Rob to climb the 1000m ice gully on the East Face of Mount Colonel Foster in a range close to his home on Vancouver Island, but still with a two day approach. The main part of the gully was 750m of black ice, constantly threatened by powder snow avalanches from the upper snow basin. It was like an extended version of Point Five Gully on Ben Nevis but here we had the additional problem of sack hauling as well. At the end of the second day we were fully committed, climbing through swirling spindrift in a major storm and desperately searching for a bivouac site, when unexpectedly we found the ideal place in a scoop of snow under a rock overhang. Next morning we awoke to find the sun shining directly into our eyrie and, after a brief tussle on one final ice pitch, we gained the summit which was bathed in morning sunlight. This provided a stupendous view of the Coast Range stretching away to Alaska in the north, the Rocky Mountains to the east and the smaller but no less interesting peaks of Vancouver Island close at hand — enough to keep Rob and his friends occupied for years to come.

The Rishi Gorge – entry to the Nanda Devi Sanctuary

Martin Boysen, Dougal Haston and I joke at our Changabang Glacier camp prior to the ascent, while Tashi busies himself with his equipment.

CHANGABANG, 1974

One of the biggest satisfactions of our Changabang climb, apart from making the first ascent of such a fine virgin peak, was the opportunity to view the fabled Nanda Devi Sanctuary with its fine peaks and its unique access route by the Rishi Gorge. We had originally hoped to climb the mountain from the Rhamani Glacier but the routes there looked too hard, so we crossed the difficult Shipton's Col and entered the Sanctuary and made the ascent from the south side. Although the route was not too hard, as we gained height it opened up fine panoramic views of the whole Sanctuary.

Changabang's reputation stems from its sharp profile as seen from the Rhamani glacier, but it looks less savage in a southerly view (*inset*) from high on Nanda Devi. Our route took a rising line across the face of Kalanka (the right-hand peak) to the saddle and then followed the East Ridge (*below*) to the summit.

PIK LENIN, PAMIRS, 1974

Nearly two hundred climbers from nine nations took part in this International Mountaineering Meet in the Pamirs. Some remarkable climbs had been done in this range, particularly extended mountain traverses at which the Russians excel, but on the accessible and popular Pik Lenin few attempts had been made to break away from the conventional routes. Thus various groups set out hoping to do new routes. Both the French and British parties made new lines up Brenva-like spurs on the North-East Face during their ascents of the mountain and the Americans did a new climb on Peak 19.

The main impression of this trip was of the regimented methods of the Soviets and their interest in competitive climbing. Climbing groups were directed by the veteran alpinist, Vitali Abalakov, and most were strictly regulated, their progress monitored using radios so that rescue parties knew their positions at all times. When bad weather and avalanches (some triggered by earth tremors) intervened these precautions often counted for little. By the end of the meet there had been thirteen deaths in four separate incidents, the saddest being the demise of eight Russian women near the summit of Pik Lenin.

(*below*) Vitali Abalakov surrounded by admirers. He made the second (and first Russian) ascent of Pik Lenin (by a new route) in 1934 and, possibly because he was not a Muscovite, escaped the Stalinist purges that decimated the ranks of Soviet mountaineers at that time. Since then he did numerous hard climbs on the great Soviet peaks and became the USSR's most famous mountaineer. He was still going strong in 1973, despite severe frostbite injuries.

(*above*) Soviet climbers wait in regimented ranks for the opening ceremony to begin. (*below*) The opening ceremony, with flag raising and other nationalistic trappings that had much in common with the Olympic Games. Disorientated, we were left drawing lots for who should be leader.

(*below*) Even the normally disparate American climbers, visiting the USSR in the wake of President Nixon's visit to Moscow, felt the urge to adopt a team strip of funky denim caps and red duvets.

(*above left*) Pik Lenin from the camp, with the Krylenko Pass on the left and the North-East Face to its right. (*right*) The Krylenko Pass, crossed several times during the Meet, was swept by a huge slab avalanche during the earth tremor. This was the route taken by the Rickmer Rickmers party on their first ascent in 1928 – from the pass Karl Wien, Eugen Allwein and Erwin Schneider followed the East Ridge to the summit.

The English and Scottish teams climbed Pik Lenin by this snow ridge on the North-East Face. (*inset*) Paul Braithwaite confronts Lenin on the summit.

A photomontage of the greatly foreshortened South Face of Denali. Our route gained the snowfields above the ice cliffs by the couloirs slanting up from the right. The lower part of the face is hidden behind the intervening ice-fall.

Dougal Haston and I with our small cache of equipment before our air-lift to the foot of Denali.

DENALI, SOUTH FACE, 1976

From Anchorage in Alaska, in late April, we were flown in to a glacier seventeen miles from Denali. We then spent four days humping food and equipment up to a base in a recently vacated igloo near the foot of the face, and a further day getting the first two pitches climbed. The air was so clear that it was hard to grasp the scale of the 3300m face and it was only after the first full day of climbing that the enormity of our undertaking became clear. The logical line on the lower face followed the 1967 route but at half-height we planned to break away to the left and head directly for the upper snow basin and the summit.

Dougal leads during a snow fall on the first day. With a thin layer of powder snow lying over ice the slopes were both difficult and dangerous. Soon after taking the photo we were both swamped by a powder snow avalanche and only saved because we had belayed to several ice pegs, which were left wilting.

(*above*) The view down the face from a ridge just below our first bivouac site. (*below*) Our safe but cramped first bivouac site where we spent two nights. Dougal did the cooking from the tent sac, while I survived in the open.

(*above*) On the third day, after traversing an avalanche chute just left of our bivouac site (under the rock buttress below), the route continued up a narrow icy couloir (left).

DENALI, SOUTH FACE (continued)

The route was committing, long, strength-sapping and often dangerous. After two nights sitting out storms on the first bivouac site most of our down gear was wet. We abandoned equipment and food in an effort to move faster. We spent the next night on a windswept ridge and had three more bivouacs (two in snow holes, the final one near the summit). On the descent we met the frostbitten climbers and then went down to spend a night at a camp at 4260m, before reascending to 5200m the following day to assist in the rescue. We thus completed eight days of sustained climbing after leaving the igloo.

In bitterly cold conditions we crossed the windswept summit of Denali and began the descent.

Mount Kenya is approached through the full range of climatic zones: parkland, dense jungle and then onto the boggy open moorland, studded with the giant groundsel plants typical of the area, from where one can admire the mountain's arresting architecture.

EAST AFRICA: MOUNT KENYA AND KILIMANJARO, 1976

A visit to East Africa provided a wonderful climbing holiday at the end of the year for Paul Braithwaite and me, as memorable for the wild life and flora of the approaches as for the climbing above.

Our attempts to reach the great icicle of Kilimanjaro's Breach Wall by a direct line up the gullies below proved too dangerous so we climbed the mountain by one of the conventional routes.

However, we made two very interesting climbs on Mount Kenya. The peak has two contrasting faces. The south-western (above and right) is more icy and dominated by the Diamond Glacier and Diamond Couloir creating a neat division between the summits of Batian (left) and Nelion. We repeated the 1975 Chouinard/Covington direct finish to the Diamond Couloir, which in these wintery conditions was serious because of the difficulty in finding good belays. The inset photo shows Paul, an outstanding ice climber, at work on one of the harder pitches.

(*below left*) The south-western side of Kibo (5895m/19,340ft), Kilimanjaro's highest peak and the highest point in Africa. The Breach Wall icicle is obvious on the left. (*below right*) Mount Kenya (5199m/17,085ft) from the west.

A brew stop in the basin below the Grey Corner.

Climbing the right wall of the Grey Corner.

MOUNT KENYA (continued)

Our best climb was a new rock route up the North-East Face of Nelion (*left*) based on the obvious Grey Corner high on the walls to the right of the North-East Pillar. We climbed a series of hard new pitches to reach the corner which provided a fine jamming cracks up its right wall, with a 5c crux around a large block overhang near the top.

(*above*) In the forests of the Homathko Valley at the end of the first day. In 1893 Alfred Waddington's road construction plans for the valley were violently rebuffed by Chilcotin Indians who killed members of a survey party in their camp while they slept.

The Homathko River.

On the South-East Ridge with the Tiedemann Glacier beyond.

MOUNT WADDINGTON, CANADA, 1978

Rob and Laurie Wood, Steve Smith, Janine Caldbeck, Ross Nichol, Jim Allan, Claude Ruel and I set out from the head of the Bute Inlet to climb Mount Waddington. The powerful impact of that rugged approach march is an abiding memory from this trip. Carrying 85lb loads we managed just five miles on the first day before camping, shattered, in dense rain forest. Three more arduous days followed, clambering up the steep forest slopes, slithering over the boulders of the Homathko River Canyon and then trudging up the moraine debris of the Tiedemann Glacier where we donned skis to complete the journey to our Base Camp. After all this effort we were still at just 1300m leaving 2700m of complex mountain terrain still to be climbed.

The north-eastern slopes Mount Waddington.

(*left*) As we prepared to leave our first bivouac the cold valley air produced a rising sea of icy mist which covered all but the highest peaks.

The final towers. The obvious snow ramp leads across to the South-East Face.

MOUNT WADDINGTON

The Wiessner/House 1936 first ascent route was from the south, but many of the later ascents have been from the Tiedemann Glacier/north-east side. Half the party took a rising line to the upper slopes of the Bravo Glacier while the rest of the us tackled the South-East Ridge. We reunited at a snow cave bivouac below the final rock towers. But the weather was deteriorating and with success looking unlikely the general mood was to withdraw. Rob Wood and I made one last try, climbed the final chimneys fast enough to reach the summit in a day, and thus completed a remarkable climb in a fabulous and remote area.

(*right*) Rob Wood moving up to the South-East Chimney, first climbed by the Americans Bill Long, Ray de Saussure, Oscar Cook and Dick Houston during the third ascent in 1950. At this time of the year it was heavily iced and strenuous with (*inset*) steep sections to overcome chockstones.

6 Ordeal on the Ogre

The Karakoram is a harsh, unforgiving land of rock and ice, further north than the Himalaya, beyond the reach of the monsoon, the soils are thin and growing things rare. But on July 21, 1977 the early morning sun shone down on one little oasis of lush green grass covered in spring flowers, buzzing with insect life, protected from the mountain winds by converging moraine on two sides and by the rocks below the Ogre's Thumb on the other. The snow on the rocks above had started to melt, filling the stream that meandered across the campsite. The heat from the sun was penetrating my soggy sleeping bag; my aching and emaciated body luxuriated in that steamy cocoon of drying feathers. It was so utterly peaceful. It was now nine days since I had broken my legs just below the summit of the Ogre, or Baintha Brakk (7285m/23,900ft), and four days since Chris had broken two ribs and got pneumonia. Waiting for the stretcher party to reach our remote spot there was plenty of time for me to go over events.

Early in the expedition, whilst attempting the Central Spur, I had managed to dislodge a rock which ricocheted down a steep gully and hit Paul Braithwaite on his thigh, putting him out of effective action for the rest of the trip. Meanwhile Mo Anthoine and Clive Rowland, Chris Bonington and Nick Estcourt were pushing fixed ropes up the steep rock and ice ribs to the left of our pillar. Mo and Clive eventually reached the top of the ribs just below the Western Col, then dropped back to the camp. But early the next day Chris and Nick unexpectedly took off with the intention of reaching the Ogre's main summit. After several days' hard climbing, with Nick becoming increasingly exhausted and ill with a throat infection, they settled for the lower West Summit, realising they did not have enough technical climbing equipment or gas to sustain an effort on that steep final tower.

It had been an incredible effort, but the feeling among the rest of the team was more resentful than congratulatory. Chris and Nick believed the arrangement was always fluid and allowed them the freedom of action to break away for an alpine-style push at any suitable moment, and anyway they had asked the others to join them. Mo and Clive had a different view as all four climbers had been working together for ten days. They needed a rest day so when Chris and Nick left them they felt very let down. Chris's competitive reputation did not win him the benefit of the doubt down at Base Camp. Clive addressed some well chosen epithets at him and eventually that cleared the air.

While these two had been on their attempt, Clive, Mo and I had been

(left) Mo Anthoine, Clive Rowland and Paul Braithwaite enjoy a well earned afternoon tea break at Camp 1 on the Ogre. Ropes were fixed up to this point and beyond to the snow plateau, and we carefully stocked three camps before making a concerted bid for the top. During the whole of this build up period the weather was excellent and as we gained height we enjoyed increasingly fine views of the intricate chains of peaks that radiate from this important region in the centre of the Karakoram.

preparing for a more technical route on a steep buttress leading to the West Summit and were now poised to set off, but Chris persuaded us to wait for him to get his second wind and join us. Nick opted out with a bad throat. So this left the four of us to make a second but more technical ascent of the West Summit, first using the fixed ropes, then taking a route directly up the rock buttress of the South-West Ridge. After crossing the West Summit we dropped down to the col between it and the main tower, where we dug out a big snow cave at around 7000m. The next morning Chris was up early with porridge cooked as I awoke and we set off first. He was going very slowly and asked me to lead. We had two rope-lengths of quite hard mixed climbing to reach some pinnacles before traversing down and across to the final rock wall barring the way to the summit.

It was now mid-afternoon. Mo and Clive had started late and were filming our progress from the pinnacles. Later they retreated when they realised our progress on the final tower was slow. Chris had obviously not recovered from his previous attempt, and I told him I thought I ought to lead the next pitch, as it looked strenuous and I was still feeling relatively fresh. He didn't object. It proved to be a very enjoyable forty-

Battered and nearly bowed, Chris Bonington (*above*) and I (*below*) recuperating in Base Camp after our desperate retreat from the mountain, Chris with broken ribs and anxious about incipient pneumonia, I with broken legs and bruised knees after days of crawling. All the pain-killing drugs had been taken down by Nick and the porters, so we had a miserable wait, albeit in delightful surroundings, until a rescue party arrived.

five metres of VS granite. I then traversed across to belay beneath the final blank wall. Chris showed no inclination to lead, so I started climbing up a crack, which went mostly free but with some direct aid from nuts and the odd peg. Eventually the crack petered out and I had to ask Chris to lower me down so I could start a pendulum to reach another crack higher up on the right. After galloping backwards and forwards the arc of my swing was sufficient to allow me to get established in the crack, put in a peg, and continue up to the top of the wall.

Chris came up raving about the quality of the climb and the exposure. It was the hardest climbing I've ever done at that altitude, on superb brown weathered granite. An overhang barring the way to the final snow gully was overcome using combined tactics where I stood on Chris's back. I reached the top just as

the sun disappeared below the horizon. As Chris followed I had time to enjoy just being up there in the middle of the Karakoram, surrounded by glaciers and other granite peaks as far as the eye could see. But even as the first superlatives were flowing out of Chris's mouth, I was hustling to get us down before it was totally dark. We had no sleeping bags and only very light clothing under our wind-suits and a forced bivouac held no attractions.

A few feet down from the summit I fixed an abseil, roped down and realised I could save time by clipping into a couple of pegs Chris had left in at the top of the wall. To reach them I had to tension across some water-streaked rock. But in the cold night air the water had turned to verglas, my feet skated off and I went out of control, turning, spinning, crashing across the rock. I put my feet up like a pair of buffers ready for impact on the rocks on the other side of the couloir. I slammed into them, lost my glasses and ice axe and came to a halt dangling on the end of the rope. As I tried to manoeuvre myself onto a tiny ledge I realised I'd broken both legs at the ankles.

Chris abseiled down and took over, continuing down to a snow patch where we spent a bitterly cold night massaging each others' toes to ward off frostbite. It was almost as bad as Everest. Next morning I was

The Ogre has still only had one ascent because it is so well defended on all sides by steep walls of rock and ice. The most reasonable point of access is on this south-west flank. The huge rock prow of the Central Spur on the right is capped by the ice slope of the South Face. We attempted both these lines but our eventual route took the mixed rib slanting up left of the Central Spur to the lowest point of the snow plateau. It then took the rock buttresses of the West Ridge on the left-hand skyline to the West Summit, went down to the col where we had a snow hole bivouac, and then finished up hard rock pitches on the main summit tower. The peak on right is Pt 6960, the western summit of the Latok group.

relieved to be able to get my boots back on and, after several abseils, we came to the point where we had to traverse across steep snow to the snow cave. Chris went ahead to alert Mo and Clive who came out to dig great bucket steps to assist me as I crawled back.

Then followed storm and starvation. For two days the blizzard pinned us down in the cave. On the third we knew we had to set off regardless, before we lost all our remaining strength. Clive led up steep and drifting snow to the West Summit and by this supreme effort got us out of the trap we were in. He and Mo left a rope for me to haul myself painfully up through the deep new snow and Chris brought up the rear. Then it was a sequence of nightmare abseils and bucket steps as I started to wear out the knees of five pairs of overtrousers. At one point I abseiled off the ends of the rope but instinctively grabbed hold of the fixed rope to prevent a record descent to the glacier. But Chris managed to break a couple of ribs after making the same mistake and later contracted pneumonia which must have been more painful than my ankles. In total it took us eight days to make it back to the moraine. I arrived last, crawling in to Base Camp at 10.30 p.m. Chris came out to meet me. 'No one else but you could have made it back,' he said. I doubt that, but it was nice of him to say so.

As soon as we were safely installed, Mo rushed off to catch up with Nick and

Paul who had left to raise a search party. He and Paul then went on to Skardu to arrange for a helicopter and to make sure news that we were safe got back to England. Five days later Nick arrived with a team of Balti porters and enough poplar wood poles to make a stretcher. Our little band proceeded down the steep moraine-covered glacier with an ailing Chris walking alongside.

Our trials weren't entirely over. The helicopter for me landed on time on a flat field two miles upstream from Askole, but crashed-landed at Skardu when the engine failed. It therefore took another seven days to bring Chris out from Askole where he was beginning to think he'd been abandoned.

Looking back fourteen years on, I can see that after Everest I thought I was invincible, could do anything. I was far too arrogant. I remember standing at the bottom and thinking as I looked up at the Ogre, 'Right, I'm going to get this body from this grass to the top of that mountain whatever happens.' Then again, I had let my long-standing differences with Chris get to me. I had passed judgement on him for leaving Clive and Mo on the first attempt. There was never the rapport on the climb that there should have been for something as serious as the Ogre. I let myself get distracted from the climb and from being totally in tune with the mountain. Indulging in passing judgements on others is perhaps the worst thing I can do and the thing I'm most prone to do. There was just no acceptance of what is – and that almost killed me.

The Baltis of Askole

During this retreat I had ample time to contemplate the skills of the Balti porters who were carrying me and on whom we rely to transport our equipment into the Karakoram. Most of them live in Askole, the last village below the Baltoro and Biafo Glaciers. This has a basic, earthy character and its four hundred inhabitants seem to reflect this – the buffs and browns of their clothing echoing the mud and adobe homes they live in. At 3000m they eke out a living at the frontiers of permanent existence. During the five months of winter they virtually hibernate below ground in their houses. After the snows have melted comes the season of ploughing and sowing on their meagre terraced fields, which are skilfully irrigated by long leats leading down from the glacial torrents. By the time the climbing expeditions are leaving the fields are emerald green with the fruits of their labour, sometimes with a surplus of vegetables or gritty flour available for sale or barter. The village sits well on a moraine terrace with cliffs to the north and out of sight and sound of the thundering Braldu far below. The arresting peak of Bakkor Das shimmers far above. Stately poplar trees lend the village a certain tranquillity. A Shangri-La? Not exactly. Not where child mortality is fifty per cent, where women look twice their age under the stress of child-bearing and work in the fields, and where gastro-enteritis is rife.

The Baltis are Shiites, followers of the late Ayatollah Khomeini, but here religious zeal is tempered by the land and climate and also by ancient Tibetan influences. The men also work hard tending flocks of goat and sheep, hunting and now, increasingly, portering – a back-breaking and dangerous occupation but financially rewarding. And the rewards are justified for these men carry awkward and heavy loads all day across punishing terrain often in appalling conditions. They have a reputation for hard bargaining to the point of striking but, if treated with respect and kindliness, expeditions will find them as loyal and hard working as the Sherpas of Nepal. Without the Baltis very few peaks would be climbed in the Karakoram.

(*above*) On the first West Ridge buttress with the Sim Gang Glacier and the Hispar peaks beyond.

(*right*) The upper part of the West Ridge just below the West Summit. Mo and Clive follow, having filmed our progress from below.

THE OGRE, 1977

Paul Braithwaite was injured on our approach to the Central Spur, so I had joined Mo and Clive to prepare the route to the West Ridge. Chris Bonington and Nick Estcourt ran out of steam on the South Face and, with Nick tired and ailing, Chris joined us for a second summit bid. We set off from Camp 3 at the foot of the ridge, hoping to climb the rest of the mountain in one lightweight push.

Mo Anthoine

Clive Rowland

(*above*) After breaking my legs in a mishap during the first abseil from the summit, the descent became a prolonged test of will-power and survival instinct, first jumaring over the West Summit (*top left*), then crawling or abseiling down the steep sections and, worst of all, the final three-mile crawl (*right*) down the glacier and moraines to reach Base Camp. It was a severe lesson which I was lucky to survive and am not anxious to repeat.

(*top inset left*) The 250m summit tower of the Ogre from the West Summit. This provided several difficult rock pitches, including one (*main picture*) that involved HVS (5.8) free climbing, some aid and a 12m pendulum between crack systems. (*lower inset left*) Chris follows the hard pitch. The South Face he had climbed earlier with Nick sweeps down below.

Galen Rowell's superb aerial view of the Ogre/Latok group showing the Uzum Brakk Glacier leading round to the Ogre with the Latok peaks on the right. Our Base Camp was just by the glacier junction on the bottom left of the picture.

THE OGRE (continued)

The remoteness of the Ogre, and the time that it took before the porters returned to help us out, was a reminder of how much we depended on local assistance in this harsh land. The Baltis have a reputation for awkwardness but, providing they are treated with respect, they are just as hard-working and loyal as the Sherpas of Nepal. Yet they have far less to be happy about, as survival in this arid terrain is a constant struggle. The high infant mortality rate in Askole is due partly to villagers drinking water that has passed through fields fertilised with human and animal excrement. It is hoped to pipe spring water in soon to prevent this.

(*left*) Balti porters carrying me into Askole after a two-day march.

(*above*) Laden Balti porters fording a river. (*below*) Load-carrying on the glacier.

(*left*) The fields of Askole. (*right*) All cooking and washing water is taken from this pool just above the village.

7 1979 – A Good Year

Kangchenjunga, Kusum Kangguru and Nuptse

Fresh from success on Everest, the idea of climbing on Kangchenjunga (8598m/ 28,208ft), the world's third highest mountain, grew in my imagination. I wanted to try a new route up the North Ridge which would require an approach through Nepal but the Nepalese government had never allowed anyone to go in to this peak from the west. At last, after years of diplomatic string-pulling, I received permission to tackle the mountain in 1979.

I invited Pete Boardman and Joe Tasker along, both of whom were already adept at lightweight Himalayan climbing. The fourth member of our small team chose himself. In Skardu, on the way to K2 in 1978, a jeep screeched to a halt and a chap with a mop of black hair and a huge smile leapt out. He said, 'I am Georges Bettembourg. I will climb with you one day, but now I am off to Broad Peak – goodbye!' And he disappeared down the road in a cloud of dust. Georges climbed all but the last few yards of Broad Peak in just a few days with

(*below*) Georges Bettembourg, Chamonix guide and scion of the celebrated Charlet family. Both skilled and effervescent, he played a key role on the Kangchenjunga climb and was later my partner on expeditions to Kusum Kangguru, Nupste, Shivling and Makalu.

Yannick Seigneur. There were not at that time many who had climbed above 8000m alpine-style so Georges was enlisted.

During our approach march we passed through country new to us, heading east through a succession of villages to the Sherpa enclave around Ghunsa. The only mishap of the walk in was when Georges gave Pete a playful shove while they were bouldering and he damaged an ankle ligament which took a month to heal fully. After Ghunsa we continued up into the mountains, passing under the huge walls of Jannu, to establish our Base Camp below the North-West Face. During the next two weeks we pushed supplies along the avalanche-raked, upper Kangchenjunga Glacier, and up a steep west-facing wall of rock and ice to the North Col at 6890m. This section of the climb was very difficult, reminiscent of the North-East Spur of the Droites, so we fitted it with fixed ropes. Above the Col we extended the route up the North Ridge and established a camp in a big ice cave at 7400m as a jumping-off point for the upper part of the mountain.

The main feature above was the Great Terrace, an extensive easy-angled ice and scree slope that led across to the final pyramid. But the Terrace was at the height of the 100 mph westerly jet stream that had battered the mountain for weeks. There was no chance to bivouac, so we headed for the frontier ridge

Nima Tenzing, who had been on the 1955 expedition, returned to Kangchenjunga twenty-four years later to help us ferry loads to the North Col. He was hit in the chest by a stone, after which I resolved never again to ask Sherpas to work in dangerous places. Nima was one of those basically kind Sherpas written about in the old books, reliable, self-effacing and cheerful in adversity. They still exist.

Ang Phurba, our sirdar on Kangchenjunga, is one of the new breed of entrepreneurial Sherpa, who now runs three tea houses in Khumbu and is operations manager of the Trekking Co-operative based in Kathmandu. He carried our summit tent to Camp 6 on Everest and in 1977, on a Korean expedition, aborted his own summit bid when close to the top to help down an ailing climber, but later reached the top on two separate expeditions. He climbed Kangchenjunga in 1980 with a Japanese expedition.

above. On the relative shelter of the Sikkim side of the ridge we hacked out a platform on a slope that dropped sheer to the Zemu Glacier. But during the night the wind changed direction, the centre fibreglass hoop of the tent snapped, and I held the billowing wreckage just long enough for Pete and Georges to evacuate our equipment before the whole tent was swept off into Sikkim.

At 4.30 a.m., in the teeth of the storm, we had to crawl and claw our way back up the twelve metres to the ridge and into Nepal and then descend five miles and 3000m back to Base Camp to recover. We reached it by 3 p.m. but then we did get off to an early start! It had been the closest call I've ever had, the finest line I'd drawn between being here and not being here, and yet it was curiously exhilarating. During the struggle I was transformed from one state of being into another, transcending the ego and freeing energy to face the unknown with adrenalin running high – wonderful stuff.

On our second attempt on the mountain, this time with Joe making up the foursome (having not been fully acclimatised for the first try), our intended lightweight push in moonlight was thwarted by the onset of darkness and driving spindrift. Georges had kept going for a period up the rocks above the Great Terrace and Pete followed him until they were forced to bivouac and eventually retreat. Back together at the ice cave we considered our next move. Georges was all for going down to recover and the others favoured getting more supplies from the col. Could a big mountain like Kangchenjunga really be climbed by just four people anyway? What if one of us got oedema? And how were we to cope with the winds? Georges didn't trust the winds, and he admitted he had shot his bolt on his nocturnal attempt.

In the night I suddenly awoke with a compelling inner feeling that we should go straight back up the mountain. At 5 a.m. I lit the stove, made a brew and woke the others. Joe, who had done seven years in a Jesuit seminary, wasn't at all impressed by my revelation. But Pete thought about it and eventually discovered an extra gas cylinder that had got buried, which made him enthusiastic. Nothing could persuade Georges, however, and he packed and descended. We set out climbing up through the rocks and onto the Great Terrace where we were elated to find that it was dead calm. As we moved across the Terrace I took the precaution of making cairns on the more prominent boulders in case we had to return in mist. We spent the night in the cave that Georges and Pete had discovered on their push. Next morning we set off optimistically at 8 o'clock, made good progress through a rock step and then plodded methodically up a band of snow that cut diagonally across the face. This led to the Pinnacles on the West Ridge which marked the point where the 1955 route came up from the other side of the mountain. It was marvellous to be up on the ridge, with only Jannu and Kabru poking out of the clouds, after being contained for weeks on the north-west side of the mountain.

The climbing was interesting and we were all in good form at the same time, Joe having now fully acclimatised. We passed below Brown's famous crack, taking the Hardie/Streather variation round into the gully leading up on the right. As the evening shadows lengthened we arrived at the top, stopping a few metres below the highest point. A lone raven circled above us, flying higher than Everest. Neither the British nor the Indians (who made the second ascent) stood on the actual summit in deference to the people of Sikkim who believe their gods reside there, so it remained the untrodden summit.

It was the first time that one of the big three peaks had been climbed

Nima Tamang, our 'kitchen boy' on Kangchenjunga in 1979. In 1985 the Americans Chris Chandler and Cherie Bremer-Kampf took him as a third climber on their ill-fated winter attempt on the North-West Face. Chandler died at 8000m and Bremer-Kampf and Nima (who had little technical climbing experience) suffered severe frostbite during an epic retreat. Sadly, Nima died in an avalanche on Everest in 1987.

(*below*) Georges Bettembourg climbing old Yugoslav ladders leading to the Lho La.

lightweight by a small team without others being there with oxygen and it confirmed my belief that these big mountains could be climbed in a far simpler manner. I could not see why all my future climbs shouldn't be done in this way.

Two and a half months later Georges and I were back in Nepal, this time hoping to traverse Everest by the West Ridge from the Lho La, and descending by the South Col route. We planned to acclimatise on Kusum Kangguru and Nuptse. Mike Covington, with whom Joe Tasker and I had attempted Nuptse the previous year, joined us for this training programme, and we hoped that Rab Carrington, Brian Hall and Al Rouse, who were climbing Kang Taiga, might later make up the Everest party. In addition, my wife Jan, with our daughters Martha, aged seven, and nine-month-old Rosie, would come as far as the various base camps.

We completed our ascent of the North Buttress of the North Summit of Kusum Kangguru in September and moved up to Everest Base Camp. Nuptse (7879m/25,850ft) was first climbed from the south in 1961 but we were hoping to make the first ascent from the northern, Western Cwm side, using an approach up the Khumbu Ice-fall. After an initial trip into the Western Cwm to establish an Advance Base Camp, Georges and I climbed to the Lho La to inspect Everest's West Ridge and assess the steepness of Nuptse's North Buttress. Following this excursion social obligations intervened, as I fulfilled my promise to be best man at Mike's wedding to Chumjee Sherpani in Khumjung.

When I got back to Base Camp it was mid-October. A depleted team of Georges and myself, with Al Rouse and Brian Hall, set off for a three-day push up the North Buttress. We were all very fit and the climb, though hard, was completed in a rapid and orderly fashion. It was very interesting to be able to look across to the South-West Face of Everest from the summit of Nuptse and also along the corniced ridge stretching out invitingly to Lhotse.

After another bivouac we descended to the Western Cwm, congratulating ourselves on what had been a perfect climb. But we were in for a shock. Looking down into the Ice-fall, we realised there had been a tremendous movement. At the top, where the ice had pulled away, we could see right down to the bedrock. There were ladders and ropes at crazy angles, none of which we could use. It took us a whole day of sustained ice climbing in a maze of crevasses and ice cliffs, constantly menaced by sérac collapse, to make a descent that can normally be done in an hour. We were all shattered, both physically and emotionally, when we got to the bottom.

Four days later the Sherpas asked what we planned to do next and, after some heart-searching, we packed up and headed for home – the only expedition I know of that has booked and paid the royalty for Everest, been at the bottom of the mountain with all the equipment necessary, fit (albeit tired) and acclimatised and never actually set foot on it. Some kind of record!

Scenes on the approach march: (*above*) A family on the move with wife and husband carrying child and goods in baskets.

(*left*) A group of village children. In this border area of Nepal medical facilities are sorely stretched, and some families survive in gruelling poverty.

This Sherpani and her four children joined us on the walk to Ghunsa. I was impressed by the grace and economy with which she fed, cleaned and mothered her children – so typical of the uncluttered dignity of the Sherpa lifestyle.

(*above*) Ploughing potato fields in Ghunsa.

(*right*) The neat Sherpa village of Ghunsa, set on the valley floor among pristine conifer forests.

Sherpanis and children from the Ghunsa region.

(*above left*) Pete Boardman was carried in relay by three very small but very strong men. (*above right*) The Nepalese border post at Ghunsa. Our Liaison Officer sits on the right.

KANGCHENJUNGA, NORTH RIDGE, 1979

The eighteen-day approach march through the Nepalese hills was quite the best I had enjoyed in the Himalaya. We had superb views north-west to Everest, and Makalu and ahead to Kangchenjunga, and ample time to shed the worldly concerns of our 'civilised' life and slowly focus on the great test we had set ourselves. We were also able to observe the lifestyles of the communities we passed through, from the tenuous subsistence living of the Tamang hill people to the cheerful industriousness of the Sherpas of Ghunsa, the last permanent settlement before our Base Camp. As we checked in at the military post of this border town, our liaison officer, Lt Mohan Thapa (Artillery) told me life in the Army was very good 'except for the loud bangs', so it seemed ironic in this garrison village to see only one rifle to keep the Chinese hordes at bay. Like all our LOs in Nepal, Lt Thapa did much to enhance our visit to his country.

From Base Camp we had this panoramic view (*right*) of the North-West Face with the Kangchenjunga Glacier leading up below it. G. O. Dyhrenfurth's 1930 Expedition was brutally rebuffed here when a huge ice cliff collapsed, killing the experienced porter Chettan who had earlier warned of the danger. This was on a line up the central ice terraces that has since been used by several expeditions in the eighties. To avoid this we decided to climb, and fix ropes, directly up the steep ice and rock face to the North Col on the left and there equip and stock a camp as a jump-off point for an attempt on the ridge. We hoped to follow the ridge to reach the extensive ramp that ran across the face above the ice cliffs and then tackle the summit rocks, either by moving back to the North Ridge or working across the mixed slopes to the East Ridge on the right.

(*left*) During the final approach to Base Camp we passed the end of the Jannu Glacier and enjoyed this fine evening view of the magnificent North Face of Jannu, which must surely be a venue for high-altitude big wall climbing in the future. Tomo Cesen's remarkable solo climb of 1989 took a line just left of the steepest section.

(*near right*) An ice avalanche that swept across the Kangchenjunga Glacier shortly after we had returned from below the 900m face under the North Col. Georges Bettembourg and Joe Tasker, at work on the face, enjoyed a grandstand view.

(*far right*) Georges Bettembourg leads an ice pitch on the face below the North Col.

Georges Bettembourg leading an ice pitch on the face below the North Col, climbing reminiscent of a major alpine mixed face.

Camp 3 on the North Col – two linked tunnel tents.

Looking down to the North Col with the Twins beyond.

KANGCHENJUNGA (continued)

With Pete still nursing his ankle and Joe
having acclimatisation problems,
Georges and I led most of the lower
face to reach the North Col. The
others, including Ang Phurba and Nima
Tenzing, had the dull and often
dangerous job of belaying and jumaring
with loads in support. The climbing
was alpine TD, mainly on iron-hard ice
but with some mixed ground. The main
danger, apart from the avalanche risk
on the glacier, was from stonefall
triggered by the lead climbers and Pete
and Nima sustained direct hits. We
fixed ropes up the whole face which
allowed us to haul up enough gear and
food (including our one bottle of
'medicinal' oxygen) to sustain further
activity on the mountain.

In a four-man team it is a problem
when one acclimatises at a slower rate
than the others and at the camp on the
Col Joe felt continually unwell and
had to descend. Pete, Georges and I
went on and dug an ice cave for Camp
4 which served as a base to climb the
steep rock step called the Castle where
we fixed a further 100m of rope.

Nearing the top of the face below the North Col.

Moving up the slopes towards the Castle where we established Camp 4.

KANGCHENJUNGA (continued)

The jet stream winds that batter the upper slopes of Kangchenjunga now became a problem. We had our first brush with them below the Castle (*above*) and higher, on the Great Terrace, we were blasted by vicious gusts that made all movement a desperate struggle. Seeking some shelter we crossed a col higher on the ridge, experiencing sharp jolts of static electricity at the crest (*right*) and in the calm a few yards below the crest we erected our tent. But at 4 a.m. the wind direction changed and in the ultimate nightmare our tent disintegrated around us and, as we emerged, was ripped from our grasp and swept away into Sikkim. We literally clawed our way back over the col and at first light fought back across the wind-raked terrace (*below*) and down to Base Camp in one day.

The upper slopes, seen from the Great Terrace. From the rock buttress on the bottom left we climbed the snow slopes to the cluster of pinnacles high on the ridge to the right of the summit.

On our next attempts (with Joe now fit) we tried the slopes to the right of the North Ridge. Our try here petered out when the weather deteriorated and we returned to Camp 4 (*right*) to regroup. Two days later we tried again (without Georges who judged the new plan too risky). We were lucky, the winds abated we had three days of fine, calm conditions. From a snow hole below the upper slopes, we set out for the summit, carrying very little, and relying on speed.

Pete and Joe, now going well, heading across the upper snow bands to the Pinnacles. By stoically keeping up with the team effort earlier they were now ready and fit for the crucial bid.

A magnificent spot to pause on the West Ridge of Kangchenjunga under the Pinnacles. Yalung Kang, the West Summit of Kangchenjunga, is in the background. The last time anyone had reached this spot was in 1955 when Joe Brown, George Band, Norman Hardie and Tony Streather had come up from the south to complete the first ascents.

The second ascent of the mountain was made in 1977 by members of an Indian expedition led by Colonel N. Kumar. They climbed the mountain from the Zemu Glacier to gain the upper part of the North Ridge. From a camp at 7990m Major Prem Chand and Naik (N.D.) Sherpa reached the top (using oxygen) to complete an important new route.

We were now proud to be adding our ascent to this fine tradition.

(*above*) Moving round from below Brown's Crack, Joe Tasker descends a chimney to join me in the final couloir which gave a long mixed pitch (*inset left*) that led out onto the summit area (*below*) with Kangchenjunga South and Kabru in the background.

Beyond the Pinnacles the ground was more complex and interesting than expected. This spurred us on, and we climbed up and down couloirs, round rocky corners, under Brown's Crack, with roped pitches for the last 160m to the summit. How good it was to be climbing up there, overcoming the debilitating effects of altitude, with just light sacks instead of two oxygen bottles whose weight did not justify the contents. Between gasps we were actually enjoying ourselves.

(*right*) Boardman, Tasker and Scott – a few metres short of the untrodden summit.

Evening shadows creep up the valley below the West Wall as we descended as rapidly as possible, regaining our snow hole two hours after dark. The next day we descended to the North Col and were finally reunited with Georges in Base Camp on the third day to complete a memorable adventure.

On Kusum Kangguru's North Ridge above the difficult lower buttress. Mike Covington belays Georges, romping away over the easier ground. The old ropes, fixed to bolts, were the unsightly relics of an earlier Japanese attempt. (*inset*) Georges in our snow cave camp.

Georges climbing a steep section of the North Buttress.

Kusum Kangguru from the north-west. We climbed the lower buttress on the left, then followed the easier angled snow ridge to the North Summit. The main summit was eventually climbed solo by the New Zealander Bill Denz from the west.

To begin our autumn programme, Georges Bettembourg, Mike Covington and I attempted this fine unclimbed peak clearly visible from Namche Bazar. We tackled the North Buttress and the North Ridge and Georges and I reached the North Summit after three days of mixed climbing (Mike, feeling unwell, waited at the highest camp). The main summit, no more than ten metres higher, was at the end of 100m of fragile corniced ridge. 'How awful,' Georges said, 'to kick our clumsy boots into that beautifully wind-sculpted snow.' It also looked rather dangerous, so we went down.

After this climb we returned to the upper Khumbu valley where I stayed with Ang Phurba and his wife. Theirs was one of the few houses with a stove and chimney (*below*). The usual smoke-laden Sherpa interior keeps down woodworm but is bad for eye and chest infections. Ang Phurba's wife not only looks after their five children but, during his long absences, keeps an eye on their tea houses and potato fields, while their older sons tend the yaks on the high pasture.

Terraced millet and potato fields squeezed onto all suitable land on the hillside at Phortse.

Mike Covington's wedding to Chumjee the daughter of Phurkipa, leader of the 1975 Everest Ice-fall porters.

Kappa Kelda, a renowned Sherpa artist, explains the symbolism of his art.

Ang Phurba's living room.

The Solu Khumbu had just been made a national park, with new regulations enforced by troops who were not always popular with the Sherpas.

(*above*) On the Lho La climb – moving out to the buttress from the rubble couloir. Nuptse (its North Buttress on the left) and the Khumbu Ice-fall are in the background. (*below*) Nuptse's North Buttress from high on Everest.

NUPTSE, NORTH BUTTRESS, 1979

Using the Ice-fall route of a German expedition, Georges and I established a two camps in the Western Cwm to below the North Buttress. We then spent a scary day above Base Camp climbing to the Lho La to view both Nuptse and Everest's West Shoulder. After ascending a wide rubble couloir for thirty minutes we moved left onto a rock buttress only to watch the couloir being swept by a huge rockfall a few minutes later. Then, after climbing a long steep section on old Yugoslav ladders, we were chastened to find their anchor pegs were very loose.

Al Rouse and Brian Hall joined us and immediately went to Camp 2 to acclimatise. A week later, after the Namche wedding celebrations, Al, Brian, Georges and I began the Nuptse climb. After an initial investigation of some troublesome séracs, we set out, and reached the summit ridge in three days with two ice cave bivouacs, regaining Camp 2 a day later, little suspecting the problems awaiting us in the Khumbu Ice-fall.

(*above*) On Nuptse's North Buttress high above the Khumbu Glacier flowing down the Western Cwm. We made a snow cave in the bergschrund and another at 7600m and next day climbed steep snow arêtes and slopes (*lower photos*) to the summit ridge. Huge whipped-cream-roll cornices encrusted the summit ridge (*inset – top right*), one being the highest point. We approached, but paused at the fracture line, a few yards below the crest.

Routes from the Western Cwm are problematic for small teams because of the complications of the Khumbu Ice-fall. The German and Polish expeditions had left and, with nobody passing through it every day, we found the route totally destroyed by collapsed séracs when we came to descend. The ice stream had lurched 100m downhill leaving a chaos of yawning crevasses and tottering séracs that took us nine hours to negotiate.

At Base Camp I relaxed with the family, happy to play with my children who had arrived after a careful monitored journey up from Khumjung. The others had also had enough and after a period of contemplation we abandoned our designs on Everest.

(*below*) We were forced into artificial climbing to cross the sérac barriers of the Khumbu Ice-fall to make progress downhill.

(*above*) From our final bivouac we had this fine late evening view across the Western Cwm to the South-West Face of Everest.

(*below*) The South-West Ridge of Lhotse, one of the harder sections of the cirque for anyone contemplating doing the Everest horseshoe.

Jan and Martha in Khumjung where they stayed three weeks to acclimatise. Chumjee (Mrs Covington) brings hot water for Rosie under the umbrella.

(*left*) Rosie and a Sherpani near Pheriche on the walk in and Martha arriving at Everest Base Camp (*right*) aboard a yak.

Down from the trials of the Ice-fall and back with the children.

NUPTSE (continued)

This was the first time we had brought such young children to the Himalaya. It was a lot to ask of Jan and Martha and Rosie, but we made sure their acclimatisation was very gradual and all Rosie's babyfood was brought in packets from England. As a result they suffered no physiological problems and spent four nights at Everest Base Camp (5356m), sleeping and eating well.

(*left*) Resting at Base Camp after the Ice-fall descent – I play with the children while Brian Hall sleeps and Al Rouse and Nena Holguin listen to the radio.

8 Himalayan Big Walls

1981: Shivling, East Pillar.   1983: Lobsang Spire, South Pillar.

Climbing big walls at altitude was the logical extension of the climbs in Yosemite and Baffin Island and I had already had a taste of it on the final pitches of the Ogre in 1977.

Research in *The Himalayan Journal* pointed to huge rock walls by the Gangotri Glacier in the Garhwal and a photograph of Shivling in the 1939 edition, captioned 'the Matterhorn of the Himalaya', was the inspiration behind our expedition of the summer of 1981. We walked in with hundreds of pilgrims to the source of the Ganges from where we first saw Shivling (which translates as Shiva's Penis).

Access to this region had been restricted for many years with the result that the first ascent (by the North-West Face) was made as late as 1974 by what must have been a very able team from the Indian-Tibetan Border Police. Our expedition was a joint Indo-British team under the overall leadership of Balwant Sandhu. The plan was for us to introduce the thirty young Indian climbers to alpine-style techniques and modern rock climbing equipment. Our eight-man team could then climb on and around Shivling.

Four of us, Georges Bettembourg, Greg Child, Rick White and I, decided to go for the unclimbed 1500m East Pillar of Shivling. We set off with ten days' food and a mass of equipment. The climb proved to be very demanding, as it brought together two different disciplines; first the slow, methodical big wall approach, and then what should have been the more rapid alpine climbing over a variety of terrain. Things were not helped by an accident at our second bivvy where Greg and Rick suffered bad burns from a serious explosion caused by a poorly fitted gas cartridge. Their tent was wrecked but they stayed with the climb the whole way, never flinching or calling for retreat, even though it was their first Himalayan experience.

On the eighth day we bivvied on the top of the actual East Pillar with 1500m drops on three sides. Most of the big wall climbing was now below us. It had involved some fantastic pendulums and overhangs and the rock had been good throughout. It had snowed every day, a fact which had not delayed us much on vertical rock, but slowed us to a crawl on easier angled ground where it had to be cleared. The following day we traversed the sharp ridge to the notch below the 300m headwall that barred the way to the summit.

Bad weather pinned us down here for the next two days, blasted by the winds tearing through the notch. We were down to our last few grain bars and two gas cylinders. At times like that thoughts turn to being in Base Camp so I applied the Dougal Dictum: No, I hadn't got frostbite, my body wasn't suffering, so I might as well continue until it did. No-one else voiced any down-going thoughts

(left) Shivling, one of the most charismatic peaks in the Himalaya, presents this fine north-easterly aspect towards the Chaturangi, Glacier, with a strong resemblance to the Matterhorn. The mountain rises 2000m above the glacier and is difficult on all sides. It was first climbed by the West Ridge in 1974 by Laxman Singh, Dorje, Pemba Tharkey, Pasang Tsering and Ang Tharkey, a climb that deserves recognition as one of the most noteworthy first ascents to have been achieved by a third world team. Their route was repeated three weeks later by another Indian team and in 1980 by a Japanese party. Also in 1980 three Tokyo University climbers completed a route up the North Ridge.

Shivling had become a target for the world's ambitious climbers. In 1981 we climbed the East Pillar (leading up from the left) and in subsequent years most of the other ridges on the mountain were climbed. The North-East Face (on the right) resisted several attempts (with one fatal accident) but was eventually climbed in 1986 by the Italians Enrico Rossi, Paulo Bernascone and Fabrizio Manoni after an epic eight-day ascent.

and when the good weather returned we channelled all our energies in the upward direction, now totally committed, as we were running out of pegs and doubted our ability to reverse the pendulums and overhangs below.

After our eleventh bivouac on a tiny ledge not far up the headwall, we successfully employed Friends (recently invented) to tackle loose and sometimes overhanging rock, camping that night just below the summit which we crossed the following day – our thirteenth on the mountain.

On the descent Georges and I down-climbed to the snow basin between Shivling's two summits, where we waited for Rick and Greg. Suddenly Georges exclaimed with alarm that they were off. I looked up to see first one and

Rick White, Greg Child and Georges Bettembourg jubilant on the summit of Shivling after our thirteen-day ascent.

then the other tumbling down, over rocks and steep ice and then out of sight. We rushed across the basin, expecting to find two dead bodies. First I met Greg who was complaining that he'd lost his new ice axe and then Rick who simply said, 'Well, that saved some time, Doug, didn't it?'

We continued down, using some fixed rope we found from previous expeditions. Don Whillans was waiting for us on the Meru Glacier. He was impressed that we'd kept on going through the storms for thirteen days but was shaking his head as if it was not for him. He told us two of the Indian climbers had died on Bhagirathi II and was clearly upset. The two Indians had been part of a four-man alpine-style team and Don felt that their ambition had outstripped their ability, inferring that they shouldn't have been climbing alpine-style at all. Don did not have much sympathy for alpine-style climbing in the Himalaya.

The source of the Ganges in the Gangotri mountains is a focal point for pious Hindus like this ascetic returning from a pilgrimage.

My goal for the summer of 1983 was the South Spur of K2. It would be my third visit to the mountain and the culmination of a multi-peak alpine-style expedition in which we planned to acclimatise among the Baltoro spires before moving up to Broad Peak and K2. For this Greg Child, Pete Thexton and I had our sights on the South Pillar of Lobsang Spire (5700m/18,700ft).

While the others busied themselves with training climbs we bided our time, waiting for good conditions and, after ten days of unsettled weather, eventually moved up to the col beneath the Pillar. Greg set off, leading on the only loose pitch of the climb, to belay beneath a perfect A1 crack. We took turns in leading, sack-hauling and cleaning and bivouacked that night with snow falling. Next morning Greg set off first again, and I followed de-pegging, then leading a long pitch up a dihedral. Further hard pitches followed but in the evening there were no bivouac sites so it was time to erect all three of our Porter-ledges, a tiered bunk arrangement clipped to one yellow rope.

Pete Thexton bivouacking on a Porter-ledge on Lobsang Spire. Pete, a doctor by profession, was a skilled rock climber and alpinist whose first Himalayan success was the 1979 ascent of Thalay Sagar (with John Thackray and Roy Kligfield). He later played a leading role in the winter 1980/81 Everest West Ridge attempt. Lobsang Spire gave him another first ascent, but sadly this determined climber was to die a few weeks later during an alpine-style attempt on Broad Peak.

Greg Child, veteran of many of the hardest big walls in Yosemite, totes his bat-hooking tools on the summit of Lobsang Spire after climbing the crackless final pitch.

On the third day we began up an impressive dihedral which looked hard. Greg, our big wall expert and veteran of ten El Capitan routes, took the lead using a series of hairline cracks. With knife blades tied off near the tips, and the tiniest of wired chocks, he steadily advanced, gently transferring his weight from point to point, moving slowly but surely, crossing periodically from one thin crack to another. Pete and I, using our last gas cylinder, melted snow to fill the water bottles, and packed our Porter-ledges, while every few minutes Greg called for slack – it was a considerable juggling act hanging off pegs.

We both marvelled at Greg's lead, it was at least A3 and so was the next pitch, but after twelve metres that gave way to VS crack climbing. The cracks continued, but less steeply so that ice was a problem as we neared the snow ramp below the exposed summit pinnacle. By the time Greg arrived with a heavy sack it was dark. Pete, who was leading, was now using his head torch, and moving up open chimneys and overhanging blocks. After a marvellous lead he finally gained the snow ramp and by midnight we were comfortably bivouacked.

The early morning light lit up Masherbrum at the opposite side of the valley. Above us the summit block was monolithic and offered no weakness. From the top of the snow ramp we looked round to the north side but the rock was again completely featureless, no crack or ledge to be seen. The summit was less than thirty metres above, so what were we to do? Pete and I thought the game was up as we had drawn a blank on all sides. Then Greg produced his Yosemite drill kit!

Now further progress hinged on ethical considerations. Should we leave it labelled the 'unclimbed peak', a challenge for free climbers in the future, making the statement that 'if not by fair means then not at all'? Greg muttered that 'summits were important'. He was alluding to comments made in a letter that Reinhold Messner had sent to Georges asking, somewhat haughtily, how Georges thought he had the right to join him on a climb when he had not got to the actual summits of Kangchenjunga, Broad Peak or Kusum Kangguru? We continued this high-altitude ethical debate in a light-hearted vein with me countering with Reinhold's other dictum about 'the murder of the impossible'. At the time the word 'murder' in that place seemed irrelevant, and Greg mischievously pointed out that he would only be making very small holes in a very big mountain range. So that argument won in the end.

In fact, he only drilled in about a quarter of an inch and hooked the holes with his bat-hooks. He had two, leapfrogging them up with his eyes glued to each one as he transferred his weight. Any miscalculation and the hook would do a little pirouette and Greg would surely fall. Occasionally he placed a rivet for protection, although they would only have held body weight and certainly wouldn't have stopped a fall, so the whole exercise wasn't exactly risk-free. After about three hours he had reached the top of the prow, a high shark's fin of red granite, and the top of our climb.

By mid-day all three of us were on the summit enjoying the view, quite untroubled by any ethical considerations! A giant lammergeier flew by, head cocked, eyeballing the three intruders who sat up in the sky with him. Clouds billowed round the valleys below and out of them we could see the Trango Towers to the west, while to the east Broad Peak and K2 beckoned.

That afternoon we descended rapidly via our route of ascent. It had been a fine climb but looking back I must confess that the question 'should we go everywhere?' will not go away. I will always wonder what the verdict would have been had we left that summit block untouched?

East meets West as these two gurus meet on the trail.

The Bhagirathi river, a Ganges tributary, at Gangotri village.

Gaumukh, the source of the Ganges.

We had an international party comprising British, Australians, Indians, a Frenchman, an American and a New Zealander – a combination of like-minded enthusiasts that was to become an increasing characteristic of my expeditions in the eighties. (*l to r*) Rick White, Don Whillans, Colin Downer, Greg Child, Balwant Sandhu, Georges Bettembourg, Doug Scott, Merv English and (*squatting*) Ratan Singh and Steve Sustad.

The Gangotri temple near a stone slab where King Bhagirath meditated.

SHIVLING, 1981

We approached by the pilgrim route to Gangotri, the northern point of the Hindu pilgrimage to the four sacred corners of India. The nearby Gaumukh (the Cow's Mouth), the source of the Ganges, is the holiest place, where a single dip in the icy waters is said to wash away sin and fulfil the purpose of life.

From our Base Camp at Tapovan the East Pillar threw down an obvious challenge. We spent a period acclimatising, doing training climbs with the Nehru Mountaineering Institute students. After this the expedition divided to tackle a variety of objectives: we to the East Pillar; the rest of the main group to the original Shivling route; six of the student group to Bhagirathi II.

(*below*) Shivling from the north. The East Buttress takes the left-hand skyline to the notch where we spent the ninth and tenth nights. The descent was down the right-hand skyline.

(*right*) Approaching up the pinnacled mixed ground of the lower part of the East Pillar. With the huge loads we were carrying for the big wall climbing on the steeper rock above, movement here was very difficult.

(*above and left*) By the fourth day we were deeply engrossed in sustained big wall climbing on the most monolithic section of the Pillar with the added complication that many of the cracks were lined with ice. Greg leads belayed by Georges while Rick and I jumared and sack hauled. On such difficult ground and at high altitude we advanced no more than five pitches a day and it took four more days to reach the top of the Pillar.

At the notch the weather deteriorated and a storm pinned us down for two days.

On the ninth day descending the sharp ridge from the pinnacled summit of the East Pillar to the notch.

One of the tents pitched precariously on a ledge at the notch.

Greg follows up an awkward overhanging corner on the headwall.

A view to the headwall from the col between Shivling's two summits.

LOBSANG SPIRE, 1983

Whereas Shivling's East Pillar had many alpine aspects, our climb on Lobsang Spire was a true big wall climb with a number of very technical pitches. This was one of the few remaining virgin Baltoro spires. I had studied it during our retreat from K2 in 1982 and targeted its slender South Pillar for later attention. The climb was as big as a Half Dome route, and only a third of it went free.

(*left*) The 600m South Pillar of Lobsang Spire dusted in snow. Our second bivouac was on rock so steep that it was necessary to use Porter-ledge tent platforms in a three storey set-up (*inset below*).

(*above left*) Two attempts had been made on the North-West Ridge, up the left skyline. We tackled the right-hand edge. (*above right*) Greg Child's picture of me leading an awkward off-width groove on the second day.

Greg Child aiding his way up hairline cracks at the start of day three. This 50m dihedral pitch was the most continuously difficult section of the climb.

Greg Child begins the bat-hooking on the final block while Pete Thexton belays.

The south-east (*above*) and north-east (*right*) summit facets were crackless and rivets provided scant security.

(*left*) The South Pillar. The snow ramp right of the summit monolith was reached by cracks on the edge of the Pillar.

My next rock climbing venture in the Karakoram was in 1990 when Sandy Allen and I made a three-day, 5b/5.9 rock route on one of the lesser Latok peaks above the Choktoi Glacier. This fabulous area offers tremendous potential for rock climbs of all grades in a remote setting. This view looking east from the base of our climb shows the Ogre (*left*) and unnamed peaks of the Choktoi/Nobande Sobande watershed.

9 Tragedies and Failures: K2 and Broad Peak

(opposite page) The South Face of K2 seen from high on Broad Peak. This has been the scene of many dramatic and tragic events during recent years as climbers struggled to ascend the unclimbed ridges and faces. The West Ridge is on the left, with the slope of the 1978 avalanche incident clearly visible above the intervening col on the South-South-West Ridge.

Our 1983 South Rib route slants up right from the centre of the picture to the Shoulder. We turned back at the rocks just below the Shoulder when one of our team began to suffer altitude problems. In 1986 Tomo Cesen gained the Shoulder by this line.

Also in 1986 the South Face and the South-South-West Ridge (the Magic Line) were climbed by Polish teams. Both climbs were desperate affairs with fatalities when the parties descended the Abruzzi Route (on the right skyline). Moreover the surviving members of the Magic Line team, by relying on the support of others, may have indirectly contributed to the sequence of events that led to a major disaster a few days later when five more climbers died on the Abruzzi Route in a storm.

We had looked across at the west side of K2 from the Ogre in 1977 with particular interest as we were to climb there the following year. K2 dominates the Karakoram, being much higher than surrounding peaks and steep and challenging on all sides. All its flanks are very rocky which is why it is the hardest of the great peaks. It is also a very cold mountain, being a lot further north than Everest, surrounded for a hundred miles by rock and ice mountains and with two huge glaciers grinding around its base. It attracts its own brand of savage weather. The approach march is long and arduous with portering costs about four times as expensive as in Nepal. All these factors compound the problems of getting to grips with the second highest mountain in the world. In the mid-70s the Karakoram had just been opened up for climbing after a fifteen-year lull and on K2 a fifty-strong Japanese expedition climbed the mountain for the first time since the Italian ascent in 1954.

In 1978 Pete Boardman and I persuaded Chris Bonington to go for the unclimbed West Ridge. He agreed, provided we took oxygen and sieged it. I didn't want to use oxygen, but I hoped we would be able to take off alpine-style after sieging the lower third of the mountain.

In the event the expedition was brought to a premature end. Pete and Joe Tasker were ahead pushing out the route towards Camp 2, while Nick and I took a turn at humping loads and fixing rope. I was leading across the slopes to Camp 2 when there were two shudders through the snow, followed by a cracking noise. I was plucked off as the rope came tight and I hurtled down, totally out of control. There was no fear. I registered only curiosity at being in my first big avalanche and contemplated the prospect of dying. Time was in suspension during those few seconds until I suddenly stopped – my heavy sack anchoring me firmly in the snow sufficient to snap the rope. I stood up and watched, horrified, as the avalanche, with Nick in the middle of it, poured down the cliffs to the glacier below.

The spirit of the expedition died with Nick and we called off the attempt. Before I left I went back to check the avalanche debris to ensure that Nick's body was well buried and not exposed to the ravens. Many years later our expedition doctor, Jim Duff, told me that during the walk in Nick described a dream in which I was poking around in ice blocks looking for his body.

I returned to the West Ridge in 1980 with Pete Boardman, Joe Tasker and

Dick Renshaw. Pete, Joe and I were fresh from our success on Kangchenjunga. Dick had done an impressive alpine-style climb on Dunagiri with Joe in 1975, though on the descent had got quite badly frostbitten. This time the plan was neither sieging nor alpine-style, but something in between known as capsule-style, whereby about 1000m of rope would be fixed to stock the first camp. The rope would then be pulled up and the process repeated. This has the merit that the climber severs his connection with the ground, while still having enough food and fuel to ride out a storm. It has the demerit of being extremely boring and time-consuming.

Returning across the avalanche slope that had taken Nick. The tracks in the foreground indicate my slide and how close I came to being swept away before the rope broke.

Nick Estcourt bivouacking in the Kishtwar. His death on K2 was a shattering blow, to Chris Bonington especially, and to all of us who appreciated him as a climber and for his infectious warmth and basic honesty. A fine alpinist, he had been a staunch participant on the Annapurna South Face and the Everest 1972 and 1975 expeditions.

It took ten days to stock the first camp. It was soon clear that we were taking too long, so I put it to the others that we should go from where we were alpine-style. Dick was adamant that he wasn't doing that. He didn't want to risk getting frostbitten again. Pete objected to the idea even being suggested and Joe went along with the others. We talked about an alpine-style ascent from the easier-angled southern side of the mountain, perhaps doing a new route to the left of the Abruzzi Spur, but none of the others seemed keen on that so we ended up attempting to repeat, alpine-style, the Abruzzi Spur itself. This was worse, for it was festooned with the ropes, ladders and winches of earlier expeditions.

Now ambition was beginning to intervene with Pete and Joe getting competitive towards each other and Joe seeming to resent my presence as the older more experienced climber. Dick Renshaw was immune to all this; he is the most self-contained person I've ever met, and was the emotional rock of the expedition. I agonised for days, knowing that everything had to be right for an alpine-style bid on such a big route: weather, snow conditions, the tactical plan and, above all, harmony within the group. Eventually, I decided I must leave. We parted without regret, in the circumstances it would have been unwise to stay, and I left the others to what turned out to be a very dramatic attempt on the Abruzzi. As for the West Ridge, it was climbed the following year by a Japanese expedition using siege tactics.

Three years later I organised a loosely knit team to attempt K2. This comprised several pairs of experienced climbers who would be free to attempt a variety of acclimatisation routes. After climbs on the rock towers near Urdukas, including Lobsang Spire, we moved up to K2 Base Camp to complete our acclimatisation programme with an ascent of Broad Peak.

All of us were in good shape except Dr Pete Thexton who had a bad chest cold and Greg Child who was recovering from illness. They were anxious to keep up with events and so set off for Broad Peak a day after Roger Baxter-Jones, Al Rouse, Jean Afanassieff and Andy Parkin. A day later Don Whillans, climbing with the experienced Hunza climber, Gohar Shar, and Steve Sustad and

Don Whillans, my mentor from Everest in 1972. I have always regretted not climbing Broad Peak with him in the twilight of his career as one of the world's great climbers.

I set out to follow. On our way up we met the first group romping down, happy with their success.

Steve and I were surprised when we caught up with Pete and Greg sleeping off the effects of climbing all through the previous night. Although Pete was still suffering from his chest cold, they were determined to press on. The following day Steve and I raced ahead, trying to get our camp as high as possible, having suggested to Don and Gohar that they leave their tent after a camp at an intermediate site and use our tent higher up. On the third morning we soon reached the col and had an enjoyable climb along the ridge to the summit.

On the way back down we passed Pete and Greg slowing picking their way through the little rocky outcrops of the ridge. We told them it was still a long way and wished them well. We continued down, passing Don and Gohar preparing to camp in our tent. Later, while resting at the K2 Base Camp, we received the shattering news that Pete Thexton had died of pulmonary oedema during the descent after turning back on the summit ridge.

Our first reaction was to think of home, and Don and Greg, who had been with Pete when he died, left immediately to get the news to his family. The rest of us stayed at Base Camp, pinned down by three weeks of appalling weather. When more settled conditions arrived only Andy Parkin, Roger Baxter-Jones, Jean Afanassieff and I remained to tackle the unclimbed South Rib, which after the weeks of storms was the only feasible new route possibility for an alpine-style attempt.

We made rapid progress, and during the second day worked our way up and around steep loose towers and buttresses, weaving a way that was basically safe, apart from some melting snow balconies. Our second bivvy was hacked out of snow and shaley rock at 6700m. The way ahead now seemed much easier and we relaxed, enjoying the magnificent bird's eye view of the dramatic meeting of glaciers at Concordia. The next two days required a big effort to break trail through steep deep snow and shifting spindrift blowing about in a fierce wind.

On the morning after our fourth bivouac, which was only 100m below the Shoulder on the Abruzzi Spur, Jean was not functioning properly. He said he was going blind, that his face and one side of his body were numb. He knew he must get down — it was obvious he was getting cerebral oedema. We helped him down the mountain for two days until, at a much lower altitude, he was able to glissade the lower slopes and walk back to Base Camp. Why Jean should suffer after going so well on Broad Peak is, like many things about altitude-related ailments, an arbitrary mystery. He had reached his ceiling on that day and knew exactly what he had to do. Often it is difficult to isolate the symptoms of oedema from those of general exhaustion, and we did not need reminding of the speed of Pete Thexton's death. But the debilitating effect of staying too long at high altitude is no mystery and, for myself, I knew I had been there too long. The porters had arrived and it was time to go home.

I had one further expedition to the mountain in 1987 but on that occasion the weather was so continually vile that we made no progress at all. Throughout the 1980s K2 has steadily increased its reputation for difficulty and unpredictability, culminating in the disaster of 1986 when thirteen climbers died, including Al Rouse and Julie Tullis after they had reached the summit by the Abruzzi Ridge. It seems that K2, so difficult and so rarely climbed, naturally generates greater ambition among climbers, and this adds a further insidious danger to the mountain's defences.

(*above*) K2 from the Savoia Glacier with the West Ridge on the left. In 1980 we reached the lowest sunlit rock band. In 1981 the ridge was climbed by Teruo Matsuura's expedition using siege tactics with oxygen and fixed ropes, though the summit climb was made without oxygen by Eiho Ohtani and the Pakistani climber Nazir Sabir. The South-South-West Ridge on the right was climbed in 1986 by the Poles Wojciech Wroz, Przemyslaw Piasecki and the Czechoslovak Petr Bozik but Wroz fell to his death during the descent.

(*below*) With Dick Renshaw (*left*) and Pete Boardman and Joe Tasker (*right*) during our approach to K2 in 1980.

Climbing up to establish Camp 1 in 1980, with the West Ridge above on the right.

(*left*) Joe Tasker swathed in retrieved ropes for fixing the slopes between Camps 1 and 2 and (*right*) leading a rock wall to our high point, just a few metres short of a possible campsite.

Joe's picture of me on the crest of the West Ridge above Camp 1.

K2, WEST RIDGE, 1980

We climbed directly to the West Ridge, thereby avoiding the open slope of the Estcourt avalanche accident. After two weeks of effort I felt that our capsule tactics were ineffective and, unable to agree how to proceed, we abandoned our bid. The ridge was climbed the following year by a team of Japanese and Pakistani climbers with my old friend Nazir Sabir becoming the second Pakistani climber to reach the summit of K2. He reported no great technical difficulties beyond our high point. On reflection, I think we should have acclimatised more thoroughly and then tackled the route alpine-style.

The view to Broad Peak from the South Rib of K2. The original route of ascent (that we used) was up the hanging glaciers and snow slopes on the right. The Godwin-Austen Glacier meets the Abruzzi and Vigne Glaciers at Concordia on the right, with Chogolisa, K6 and K7 the prominent peaks in the background.

Looking towards the Col from the highest camp.

Steve Sustad climbing on our second day on Broad Peak.

Our 'A team' of fast-moving climbers — Baxter-Jones, Parkin and Rouse — on the summit of Broad Peak.

(*above right*) On Broad Peak's summit ridge just above the col. The hardest part of the climb, exposed to the wind and, at close to 8000m, quite serious.

BROAD PEAK, 1983

Don Whillans told me he hoped to climb another 8000m peak before he was done. It is to my great regret I didn't climb with him on Broad Peak. But I knew from our training sorties that he was going to be slow and Steve Sustad and I wanted to climb Broad Peak, by a new direct start, and quickly, to leave enough energy for our K2 bid. Don therefore teamed up with Gohar Shar and their bid ended when they ministered to Greg Child and the stricken Pete Thexton during their descent.

Broad Peak from the west. The original route goes to the col and along the long skyline ridge to the right to the Main Summit.

Ours was not a conventional expedition, but rather a loosely knit group of friends, each with his own objectives, linked only by a Base Camp and supply structure. This allowed great fluidity of climbs and partners, but also introduced a certain competitiveness. (*l to r*) back row – Nabi (cook), Roger Baxter-Jones, Jean Afanassieff, Beth Acres, Doug Scott, Steve Sustad, two liaison officers; in front, Greg Child, Al Rouse, Don Whillans, Gohar Shah (climber and sirdar), Mohammed (cook). Not shown – Andy Parkin and Dr Pete Thexton.

K2, SOUTH RIB, 1983

After the tragedy on Broad Peak and an intervening period of bad weather the team for our K2 climb was reduced to Roger Baxter-Jones, Jean Afanassieff, Andy Parkin and myself. We were all keen to climb K2 alpine-style by a new route and the South Rib looked the ideal objective for this. Jean had gone very high on the face in 1981 with Yannick Seigneur and members of our party had gone 1000m up the rib a month earlier. We thus made steady progress, despite the deep snow after the weeks of storms.

K2 from Base Camp. The Abruzzi Spur is on the right with the South Rib the next line to the left.

(*right*) On the steep lower section of the South Rib, made more difficult by deep fresh snow.

A long-focus picture of K2's summit region. Our high point on the South Rib was just to the left of the rocks at the foot of the Shoulder.

Fighting wind and deep snow on the third day, heading to the left of the rocks.

As we got higher the deep snow and icy winds made trail-breaking very arduous. There was also some avalanche danger, so for our fourth bivouac we stopped in a safe position under rocks 100m below the Shoulder. On the fifth day, at about 7500m, Jean announced that he was suffering various symptoms of altitude sickness. With Pete Thexton's death in mind, we descended rapidly and regained Base Camp two days later, relieved to have avoided another fatality. After this Roger, still strong and keen, attempted the Abruzzi Route, reaching the séracs above the Shoulder at 8250m where bad weather forced another retreat.

IO Makalu and Chamlang

Four expeditions to the Barun Valley, 1980–1988

(*above*) Makalu, Lhotse and Everest bathed in early morning light in this long-focus view from the North Col of Kangchenjunga. The Eastern Cwm of Makalu is clearly visible and seven miles further east the North-East Ridge of Everest runs down to the right. Our objective on several trips to Makalu was to climb the shadowy, left-hand ridge up to the rim of the cwm, descend into the basin and then ascend the headwall directly to the summit. We planned to complete the climb by traversing the mountain by descending the original French route.

Looking east from Kangchenjunga three more of the five highest mountains in the world can be seen – Everest, Lhotse and Makalu – and from that angle Makalu, like a huge throne, looks far the most interesting of the three. A six-mile ridge leads from the south-east up to and along the rim of the Eastern Cwm of the mountain, a hanging valley, all of it above 7500m. The upper half of this ridge from the South Col was first climbed by Makoto Hara's Japanese expedition in 1970. It was the Eastern Cwm that fired my imagination and around it I hatched a plan of climbing the full length of the lower South-East Ridge, dropping into the Cwm, striking directly up the 600m headwall to the summit, and then descending to the Makalu La by the 1955 French route.

Makalu had such a hold on me that I was to go there four times in all. The first three expeditions in the early eighties were all to the South-East Ridge and I was lucky to be there before the advent of mass tourism and before 8000m summit craze had got under way. We had Makalu to ourselves and though the mountain was our declared objective, the walk in and acclimatisation on the surrounding peaks were equally rewarding in themselves.

My first visit was during the post-monsoon season in 1980 with Georges Bettembourg and Roger Baxter-Jones. The late Dougal Haston's* friend Arianne Giobellina accompanied us and took part in some of the training climbs. After climbing on Kangchenjunga the year before, I knew the importance of proper

* Dougal Haston had died in a skiing accident in Switzerland in 1977.

Resting after our major attempt on Makalu in 1980. It was far more satisfying than after Everest. On Makalu the media was absent. Only our three Sherpas were in attendance and they were in the same headspace as ourselves.

acclimatisation before attempting a big peak alpine-style and therefore booked Kangchungtse (7640m/25,066ft) for a training climb. We climbed four 6000m peaks and then climbed Kangchungste in five days via the Makalu La. Another plus for Makalu is having a Base Camp at 4800m, which is low enough to give the body a proper chance to recover between acclimatisation forays, far better than the Base Camps on Everest and K2 which are too high for proper recovery.

We set off from the foot of the South-East Ridge on October 14 and three days later came to a halt below the black gendarme, where we committed ourselves to dropping 300m into the Eastern Cwm through soft thigh-deep snow. Next day we finished pushing up this remote cwm and began climbing the headwall. We were now in the area of Makalu's wind plume created by the westerly jet stream, and this pinned us down in a holocaust of swirling snow for the whole of the next day. At this point Georges began to develop what proved to be a pulmonary embolism. It was clear that we had to get off the mountain fast. So we started a nightmare retreat down the cwm, spending a dreadful night at 7760m, half-way back up to the South-East Ridge, with the tent poles broken and the tent wrapped around us. Once back on the ridge we descended the steep slopes to the South Col and escaped down the glacier. None of us had previously been at such a high altitude for such a long period and we could easily have succumbed. But going to the limits of endurance on a climb and concentrating on staying alive does something to clear the clutter of trivia inside the head, creating space for inner peace. I had a profound feeling of well-being after that climb on Makalu.

A few months later a phone call from Reinhold Messner had my thoughts turning once more to the South-East Ridge. He had booked Makalu for the autumn of 1981 and was inviting me along to make a two-man team. So I

My daughter Martha had her first taste of Himalayan climbing reaching 6000m on the South-East Ridge of Makalu.

The 1000m headwall that dominates the West Face of Makalu – our target in 1988. The conditions were not good enough to tackle such a major objective, all of it above 7000m, and the face is still unclimbed.

booked Chamlang for acclimatisation and, as that was a peak only open to foreigners if accompanied by Nepalese climbers, we added Pasang, Minga and Ang Dorje to the party. Reinhold and I had already agreed to make it a family outing as far as Base Camp, with his friend Nena, who was seven months pregnant, my wife Jan, our daughters Martha (8) and Rosie (3), assorted friends, plus cook, cook boy, liaison officer and fifty porters.

Reinhold demonstrated his fitness during the first two weeks of acclimatisation and was usually a dot in the distance. But I soon acclimatised and then we addressed ourselves to Chamlang (7290m/22,911ft). This proved to be a very fine mountain. It had only had one ascent by the Japanese/Nepali expedition from the south-west in 1962. We climbed it from the north to the low point of the five-mile summit ridge and then ascended a subsidiary top at 6990m.

From the summit ridge of Chamlang we saw a UFO, a tapering box-like object, shining like tinfoil in the mid-day sun. After hovering above us it moved off very fast to the north-west. We later found that two other expeditions on Makalu had also seen it but, curiously, none of us had taken a photograph.

At Base Camp Reinhold learned that Nena, who had returned to Kathmandu, had given premature birth to a daughter. Clearly, he had to be with them, and he left in a rush, trekking all the way to Kathmandu in the phenomenal time of just three days. Fitness, speed and style are his hallmarks. At home in the Tyrol he trains intensively by running up hills carrying a heavy sack, he uses a minumum of custom-designed ultra-lightweight gear and sets off on a climb only when he is sure the weather has settled. In terms of style and careful planning Messner's Himalayan climbing is unsurpassed.

We planned a similar acclimatisation programme for our Makalu bid of 1984: an ascent of Baruntse and another route on Chamlang. This was to be the largest expedition I have ever organised with twelve climbers, including my son Michael, and ten others, including, once more, Jan and the girls.

We climbed Baruntse in one continuous twenty-two mile round trip from Base Camp. For Chamlang we split into two groups to attempt the East Ridge. I climbed with Michael, enjoying his new-found enthusiasm for the Himalaya. We took turns leading through on quite hard ice and, with Jean Afanassieff and Ang Phurba, reached the East Summit (7290m) and the Central Summit (7235m), two of the highest unclimbed tops in Nepal.

We were now ready for Makalu. Michael teamed up with Terry Mooney to attempt the original route where they hoped to meet Steve Sustad, Jean Afanassieff and me coming down to the Makalu La from a successful traverse. At first all went well. We climbed our ridge much faster than in 1980 and on the fourth day dropped into the Eastern Cwm. But on day six, our first on the headwall, we only gained 200m, so deep and difficult was the snow. The bivouac that night was a disaster. We lost a fuel canister and the tent collapsed several times under snow coming down from above. The next day we only covered another 200m and our triumph at eventually reaching the ridge was shattered by discovering the body of a missing Czech climber sitting among the snow and rocks. We bivouacked below a rock tower at 8370m. Before turning in I investigated the route left of the tower to about 100m of the summit.

Next morning we traversed out to the right of the tower and just

below the summit, but the snow was so deep we had to flounder back to our bivvy. We had run out of fuel, we all had sore throats, there was cloud above and below us. It was at this point Jean decided he'd had enough. He simply said, 'I go', and he was gone, loping down the steps of our ascent.

Steve and I followed him, knowing we could not leave him to make the descent and the climb out to the ridge alone. The next day was one of the most exhausting I have ever had in the mountains. It was with the greatest difficulty that we escaped from the Cwm, with Jean falling asleep at every rest. It was all Steve and I could do to get him to his feet and we eventually stumbled into Base Camp after a nine-day epic again at the limit of our endurance.

At first I was upset at having to give up the climb when success appeared so close. But at Base Camp I realised that Jean's instincts had been correct ... he had been in touch with that critical inner voice. He may well have saved our lives as I later discovered that our planned descent route is very complex in the mist.

In 1988 I returned to Makalu to attempt the West Face, but snow conditions were appalling and in that state the huge wall, a thousand metres of granite above 7300m, was impossible. The mountain was crowded with fifty climbers from several different nations pursuing their separate ambitions, some at the expense of others. In future I decided I would direct my attention to less populated areas.

A steady acclimatisation programme was an essential part of the plan. Chago South (*left*) on the frontier ridge provided fine views. The five-mile Chamlang massif dominates the horizon.

(*below*) The North Face of Makalu from the Makalu La. The original 1955 route went this way and we studied it carefully as our descent route on the planned traverse.

The South-East Ridge of Makalu. In 1970 the Japanese went directly to the col and then climbed the ridge, later turning the Black Gendarme which was too hard for loaded sherpas. 3000m of fixed rope was used. We crossed the satellite peaks on the right, and made our second Camp on the Japanese Col.

Georges Bettembourg and Roger Baxter-Jones stoke up at Base Camp prior to the big climb.

Approaching Pt. 6855. We climbed the steep slopes beyond to gain the ridge at the snow shoulder.

MAKALU, SOUTH-EAST RIDGE, 1980

Since the K2 accident in 1978 I had been sceptical about fixed ropes. Not only are they a negation of climbing but, paradoxically, by repeatedly moving up and down a fixed route, climbers take more risks. Our climb on Kangchenjunga was lightweight, but still had 900m of fixed rope. The capsule-style tried on K2 was unsatisfactory but the mainly alpine-style climb on Nuptse was far better. On Makalu we all agreed to try to climb the mountain using only our climbing ropes, an altogether more challenging prospect. But even here the old ropes littering parts of the route marred the enjoyment.

(*above*) Cooking at our camp on the col in the faint warmth of the evening sun. Taking a tip from the Sherpas, we lived on tsampa, enlivened with cheese and chilli sauce.

(*below*) On the steep slopes above the col.

Putting our necks into the noose as we began the descent into the Eastern Cwm, knowing that any retreat would be very taxing after a period at high altitude.

(*above*) Georges and Roger working up the Eastern Cwm. We had descended the slopes on the far right. The Kangchenjunga range dominates the horizon. (*left*) Forcing a way up the cwm to the headwall in high wind and deep snow.

MAKALU, 1980 (continued)

We climbed the windswept ridge to below the Black Gendarme where we descended diagonally for 300m to the comparative shelter the Eastern Cwm to make our fourth camp. On the fifth day we moved up to the head of the cwm and climbed the lower part of the headwall to 8079m. But the weather now got worse and the jetstream winds pinned us down in our tent next day during which Georges had stabs of pain round his liver — symptoms of a pulmonary embolism. On the ensuing retreat the 300m re-ascent to the ridge was as gruelling as

we had feared — particularly for Georges whose embolism made every step an agony.

(*below*) In our 8079m camp — Roger dozes while Georges grows anxious about incipient pains.

(*above*) On the eighth day – Georges and I carefully descending the steepest section of the South-East Ridge in a vortex of wind and spindrift.

(*left*) Fighting our way back up to the ridge to escape from the Eastern Cwm.

(*below*) On our ninth day we eventually gained the foot of the glacier after a direct descent from the col. Three days after this considerable expedition Roger was strong enough to make a four-day solo attempt on Makalu by a new line on the left side of the West Face but was foiled by high winds on the North-West Ridge.

(*above*) The locals turned out in force for a new spectator sport — watching the climbers and their friends at breakfast at the campsite outside Khambari. (l to r): Nena Holguin, Arianne Giobellina (front), Elaine Brook, Rosie and Jan Scott and Reinhold Messner.

During training excursions Reinhold, super fit, was always striding ahead.

Rosie, now a seasoned expeditioner, enjoys the view from my back.

CHAMLANG 1981

In autumn 1981 I returned to try the South-East Ridge of Makalu with Reinhold Messner. We planned a new route on Chamlang for the main training climb. This would be on the unclimbed North Face, the only other ascent having been from the south-west by a Japanese-Nepali team in 1962.

(*right*) Himalayan experts confer on a visit to the Makalu West Face expedition — Alex MacIntyre (left of Arianne), Wojciech Kurtyka, Jerzy Kukuczka and Reinhold Messner — four of the main players of the Himalayan (alpine-style) game of the early eighties.

(*above*) Chamlang from Makalu, showing the East and Central and West Summits. We moved up below the North Face (*below left*) and dug a snow cave at 6600m (*inset right*). Reinhold's first experience of snow-holing was not pleasant as he woke under a metre of snow. He soon got into his stride however, rapidly negotiating the snow flutings on the steepest part of the face (*below right*).

CHAMLANG, 1981
(continued)

Chamlang proved a satisfying mountain. Access conditions stipulated that it be tackled by teams including Nepalese climbers. On the North Face we were attracted by the elegant snow-fluted face of Pt 7205, but with monsoon snow heavy on the mountain, and with Sherpa climbers (Ang Dorje and Pasang) in the party, we opted for the less ambitious goal of climbing to the low point of the summit ridge and making the first ascent of a subsidiary summit at 7010m.

Rosie Scott and Jeanne Afanassieff in the lap of the Buddha, near Kathmandu.

Crossing the Arun by a typically rickety Nepalese bridge.

MAKALU, SOUTH-EAST RIDGE, 1984

This was one of my biggest expeditions with a cosmopolitan membership and a full support group of families and friends. This time, in addition to my wife and daughters, my son Michael came too, and he joined me on a new route on Chamlang. As a spring expedition we expected there would be less wind and for it to become steadily warmer. It was my third visit to the area and I gave more attention to points of interest on the approach route.

Above the Barun Gorge are two caves sacred to Hindu and Buddhist alike and attributed to Shiva and Parbati. Pilgrims drink and bathe in the holy water which falls from them which is said to prolong life.

MAKALU, 1984 (continued)

It was ironic that I, who had always favoured small simple expeditions, should find myself the leader of a party of twenty-five climbers, family members and trekkers. But we were really four expeditions in one, with a holiday atmosphere that was most agreeable. Our main acclimatisation climbs were on Baruntse and Chamlang, the former by the original route, to give us a chance to train the three Nepalese who would join us on what promised to be a sustained ice route on Chamlang East. Sixteen climbers set out for Baruntse but various ailments thinned the numbers during the long approach and only eight tackled the steep part of the mountain.

Some of the team: (l to r) Doug Scott, Choe Brookes, Jim Fullalove, Jean Afanassieff, (behind) Michelle Afanassieff, Michael Scott, Clive Davies, Larry Bruce, Terry Mooney: (in front) Brian Hall, Steve Sustad and Molly Higgins.

Approaching Baruntse by the Lower Barun Glacier. We made three camps on the approach and another on the mountain which we climbed by the steep ridge on the left. (inset) Ang Phurba, Steve Sustad, Jean Afanassieff, Terry Mooney and Sila Tamang on the summit.

[144] MAKALU AND CHAMLANG

BARUNTSE/CHAMLANG, 1984

We took the original Anglo-New Zealand line up the snow shoulder and South-West Ridge. An initial ice cliff presented technical climbing and above this a very steep snow slope was serious and hard. Six of us eventually reached the top. Terry Mooney was the first Irishman to climb a 7000m peak.

We then climbed Chamlang East (7235m) and Central (7180m). Ten climbers in two groups set out to tackle the North Face to reach the North-East Ridge. Choe Brookes dealt rapidly with a 17m ice cliff (right) just below the ridge, after which our group of Jean Afanassieff, Ang Phurba, Michael and I pressed on to the summit and on to Chamlang Central. I then failed to locate our 1981 route for the descent and instead committed the party to a steep ice face, with a precarious bivouac and many pitches of traversing. The other group also had their adventures with Mooney's snow blindness and an injury to Hall prompting an arduous and complicated retreat.

(*below*) the North-East Ridge of Chamlang. We took a diagonal line from the right to the shoulder and then followed the ridge to the top.

From our impromptu descent bivouac on Chamlang we had this wonderful evening view of Makalu, with the West Ridge flanked by the West Face (*left*) and South Face (*right*). Kangchungste and the Makalu La are on the extreme left and the South-East Ridge is on the right.

On Chamlang's North Face – traversing impressive icefields as we tried to find a way down.

(*above*) Michael Scott on the final climb to Chamlang Central.

MAKALU, SOUTH-EAST RIDGE, 1984

After a week's rest Steve Sustad, Jean Afanassieff and I set out for Makalu. Above the col the route was marred by the ropes and detritus of three previous expeditions which were impossible to avoid (though they did speed our retreat). Despite poor snow conditions we made steady progress and by the end of the fifth day we were nearing the top of the headwall, when we found the frozen body of a Czech climber who had been lost in 1976. He was sitting between two rocks where he had clearly stopped for a rest, never to recover.

Jean Afanassieff and Steve Sustad preparing to leave our second camp on the ridge early in the morning.

Looking up the cwm to the headwall from the Black Gendarme where we descended to the cwm.

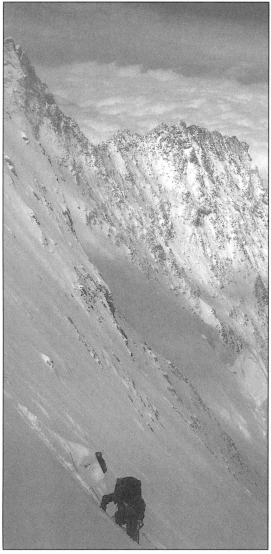

At the top of the headwall, near our high point, 150m below the summit.

Steve and Jean in deep snow on the headwall.

Steve in extremis during the retreat.

Wading up out of the cwm through fresh deep powder snow, Steve climbing and Jean slumped below.

MAKALU, 1984 (continued)

Below the summit was a steep rock tower with no obvious way forward. After a sixth camp (our third above 8000m), we tried to find a way round this to the top and the expected easier descent route. But after an abortive attempt Jean, who had become very concerned about our position, said he was going down. We had no choice but to join him on yet another hazardous retreat, with no fuel left, and all of us now dangerously tired.

The peaks of the Barun valley provide a satisfying mix of easy and hard peaks at a range of altitudes and, with wide valleys, even the most modest training peaks give spectacular views. The 8000m giants of Everest, Lhotse and Makalu tower impressively at close quarters and, to the west, Cho Oyu, Menlungste and Gaurishankar are clearly seen.

(*above*) Nuptse, Lhotse and Everest seen from Makalu's South-East Ridge. The lower peaks in the middle distance are Cho Polu and Pt. 7502.

(*right*) The South Face of Lhotse from Baruntse.

11 Climbs in Buddhist Lands

Ascents in Tibet, Bhutan and Ladakh

The Himalayan surveyors had the best job going, triangulating their way systematically through the foothills of the Himalaya, backtracking, cross-checking, projecting on from one horizon to the next, moving as self-contained units, cut off for months at a time, living off the land among the local people, filling in the blanks on the map. Through the 1980s I was fortunate enough to be able to slot in four of the more satisfyingly obscure pieces of my personal jigsaw map of the Himalaya, one I have built up since my first visit in 1967.

They are all in areas of political sensitivity which means access for foreigners has been limited. Perhaps it is this that has helped preserve their uniquely Buddhist ambience. The notorious Chinese 'liberation' of Tibet in 1949, and the later reign of terror by the Red Guards in the Cultural Revolution shut off the northern side of the Himalayan divide for decades. But while the Chinese destroyed thousands of monasteries and massacred their inhabitants, they could not win over the hearts of the people of the Great Plateau that calls itself the Land of the Religion. To the east of Sikkim lies the kingdom of Bhutan, preserving its independence and integrity with a rigorous policy of isolationism. And to the west the high valleys of Ladakh were out of bounds during a fierce on-going border dispute between India and Pakistan.

However, by the end of the 1970s doors were occasionally opening in all three areas and permission was obtained from the Chinese Mountaineering Association to attempt Shishapangma (also known as Xixabangma or Gosainthan), which is at 8046m/26,400ft, the highest mountain wholly in Tibet.

Travelling in Tibet is sobering. There are now approximately a million Chinese troops and civilians there to control no more than six million Tibetans. In the west of the country the Chinese have been testing nuclear devices, in the east they have cleared vast areas of prime forest, creating conditions that led to the flooding of Bangladesh in 1988. Some seven monasteries have now been restored, those strategically near the few permitted tourist areas.

Our piece of paper gave us permission to attempt the South-West Face of Shishapangma, but we had great difficulty in persuading our yak-drivers to lead us to this hitherto unvisited valley and not to the easier north side by which the mountain was first climbed by the Chinese in 1964 and later by a German expedition. Ours was a completely unknown face, 2750m high. After two training climbs we were fit and acclimatised and for the main ascent I was with

(top left) The restored Buddhist monastery at Gyantse. During the late sixties Tibetan monasteries were razed or pillaged in the frenzy of the Cultural Revolution. The Chinese saw that Tibetan Buddhism was an obstacle to their communist creed and their colonialism and made a determined effort to destroy it. Now the demands of tourism and belated international protests have led to a pause in this ruthless persecution. Selected shrines and monasteries are being rebuilt and small groups of monks are being allowed to return in wary toleration of a religion that the Chinese recognise as the core of the resistance to their occupation.

(lower left) The dilapidated remains of the old Tibetan town of Xegar hemmed in by the modern blockhouses and barracks of the Chinese.

(near left) A nomadic Tibetan boy listens to Pink Floyd on my Walkman

An occupation army: off-duty Red Army soldiers in Shigatse.

Alex MacIntyre and Roger Baxter-Jones, tired but jubilant during our third bivouac on Shishapangma.

Roger Baxter-Jones and Alex MacIntyre, two of the finest of the emerging generation of alpine-style climbers in Britain. We climbed Shishapangma in three very long days, going flat out, carrying all our supplies on our backs, climbing unroped on much of the ascent and descent. It was a totally satisfying climb on a major unexplored face which had pushed us to the limit.

No one I've climbed with has been stronger or more competent than Roger, and Alex was full of enthusiasm and invention, an inspiration to be with. His death from a chance stonefall at the foot of Annapurna that autumn was a shattering loss to alpine-style mountaineering, as well as to his friends in British and Polish climbing circles. Three years later Roger and a client he was guiding were killed by a sérac collapse on the Triolet North Face.

In 1987, I was back in Tibet to grasp one of the most elusive pieces of my personal Himalayan jigsaw. I had spent nine months of my life on the south side of Everest, mostly climbing its South-West Face. I had seen the foot of the West Ridge from the Lho La and, on the same trip in 1979, had a grandstand view of the original South Col route from Nuptse. I had also observed the Kangshung Face from Makalu. I was now one of a small party attempting the North-East Ridge which had repelled three strong expeditions.

Once again a long ridge proved more difficult than steep face-climbing. On a face such as the South-West Face of Everest the route is usually more direct, so less time is spent on the climb, and a face is less exposed to the winds. A long ridge is rather like being on a summit all day with the ever present risk from the chill factor being added to the sheer impossibility of making progress when the winds reach hurricane force. Snowfall clears quickly on a steep face, but on a ridge it can form dangerous cornices or simply lie so deep that climbing slows to a wallow. We knew it was never going to be easy, and the piercing wind and a record snowfall combined to defeat us half-way up the First Pinnacle at a height of 8100m.

Back at Base Camp I learnt that my Sherpa friend Nima had been killed by a freak avalanche along the yak trail. This was a great personal loss, for Nima had been on all my expeditions to Nepal since 1979 and also visited my home in England. He was the only person I know who seemed to be in perfect harmony with himself and the world. When I was leaving our Advance Base I had suggested to Nima that he use my sorbo sleeping mat. He said, 'That would be very nice, Sahib, but when you come back you will need it and, having got used to it, I will miss it, so I'd rather not bother.' He was a Buddhist through and through. We learned more from Nima than he ever did from us.

Travelling back through Tibet on the sad mission to register Nima's death in Lhasa, I could not help noticing how many more Chinese civilians there were on the market stalls, and the streets were bristling with green-uniformed military pointing their rifles at us

A colourful Buddhist celebration at the Hemis Monastery, Leh.

A professional prostrater in Lhasa. Pilgrims spend hours prostrating in penance and prayer around the Jo Khang (cathedral) but Buddhists who are too busy to pray and prostrate can hire a professional to act as their proxy.

as they patrolled. Only a few weeks later the traditional tolerance of the Tibetans exploded in riots against their Chinese oppressors and, as usual, these were ruthlessly supressed.

The Bhutanese have managed to preserve a large degree of independence. They have limited the number of visitors to their country to 2500 per annum. Unlike the neighbouring Sikkim and Tibet, Bhutan controls no important route across the Himalaya and has thus avoided annexation or invasion. In 1988 I organised an expedition to attempt Jitchu Drake (6790m/22,227ft). There had been three previous attempts on this peak. In 1983 the South Summit was reached by an Austrian team who climbed the South-West Ridge using lightweight tactics. In 1984 a Japanese expedition made a fixed rope route up the South-East Ridge. A few months later an Italian team, attempting to repeat the Japanese route, had a disaster when two of its members died when a cornice broke. The higher North Summit was still untouched.

My overwhelming impression of Bhutan was one of space and sanity. Two-thirds of the country is still covered in forest and the broad valleys boast only a scattering of hamlets. In Nepal every square inch would have been terraced, cultivated and populated, with forest cut back to the ridges and the soil eroding. We looked first at the East Face of Jitchu Drake, but soon realised our chances of climbing its snow-plastered ribs with their menacing snow mushrooms was remote. So we turned our attention to the South Face and picked a new line straight up the centre. The route provided some very steep ice climbing much of which we had to overcome in poor weather. In the end, although we were forced off the direct line, three of us made it to the top after a three-day push.

While Bhutan restricts access to Shangri-La, India and Pakistan restrict access to a war zone at the other end of the Himalayan chain on their disputed border in Ladakh. Their armies have been fighting inconclusively over the mighty Siachen Glacier for years, but recently India has allowed a few expeditions in, provided they join forces with Indian climbers under an Indian leader.

The Indian Army climbers we teamed up with in 1989 made the second ascent of Rimo IV. Meanwhile, Steve Sustad, Nick Kekus, Laurie Wood, Sharu Prabhu and I attempted the unclimbed Rimo II using alpine-style methods and, from a high camp, Sustad and Kekus eventually reached the summit. We had designs on the magnificant South Buttress of Rimo III, but to our intense frustration, the Indians called off the expedition before we could mount our attempt.

Ladakh is known as Little Tibet, and of all the Buddhist lands I visited, this seemed the most fragile, with its traditional values eroded by the infiltration of Muslim businessmen from Kashmir who were taking over the economy in the wake of the military, and by a swelling stream of tourist traffic around Leh. But despite the many difficulties, the eastern end of the Karakoram is a fine place for filling in the jigsaw, with countless mountains to be explored and climbed once the hostilities come to an end.

The Irish climber, Nick Prescott, passed his permission for this peak to me and I invited him to join the trip. The objective, an alpine-style ascent of the unclimbed South-West Face, clearly required a team of proven high-altitude climbers, so I asked Paul Braithwaite, Alex MacIntyre and Roger Baxter-Jones to come along. Elaine Brook, who was keen to see Tibet and take part in the training climbs, joined at a late stage. To reach Tibet we had to travel via Beijing which allowed us a fascinating glimpse of modern China, a sharp contrast to the nomadic and religious aspects of Tibet.

(*right*) The team on the Great Wall of China: Roger Baxter-Jones (*left*), Alex MacIntyre, Elaine Brook, myself, Paul Braithwaite and Nick Prescott.

Scenes in Beijing: (*above*) ritual swordplay, a traditional martial art still popular in China; (*above right*) intimacy in public – only recently tolerated; (*lower left*) a city of bicycles; (*lower right*) Tai chi exercises.

Scenes in Tibet: (*above*) nomadic horseman on the Tibetan steppes near Dingri; (*below*) nomads and monks brewing tea outside Tashi Lumpo Monastery at Shigatse. The left-hand figure folds his fingers in a superstitious gesture to counteract the effect of photography.

On the ridge of Pungpa Ri (7445m/24,427ft) with Nyanang Ri on the left and the aptly named Eiger Peak in the background on the right.

SHISHAPANGMA (continued)

We established ourselves at the foot of the mountain and during the first three weeks of May, in atrocious weather, carried out an acclimatisation programme which included ascents on Nyanang Ri and Pungpa Ri.

After this Roger and Alex were fit and keen to tackle the big climb but Paul had a chest infection and had to go home. Elaine and Nick found they were unable to keep up with the pace of events. There were tensions within the party and in the end Elaine decided to leave. After resolving our differences, Alex, Roger and I, supported by Nick, moved up to a high bivouac site to mount our attempt on the face. Meanwhile Wu, our enthusiastic interpreter, ferried loads. From the bivouac site we had a grandstand view of the huge face and were able to monitor the frequency of the stonefalls down the ice couloir we were to climb. It was obvious that to be safe we would have to move quickly. After paring down our food and equipment to a minimum we made an early start, hoping to make enough height to reach a bivouac above the rock band.

(*left*) Our bivouac below the face was splendidly sited above the Nyanang Phu Glacier with fine views of the Jugal Himal peaks (*left*) and the Langtang Himal peaks of the Nepal/Tibet border on the right.

(*right*) The South-West Face of Shishapangma with a telephoto (*inset*) showing the three climbers in the ice couloir on the first day.

Roger Baxter-Jones moves off the rock
rib back into the ice couloir.

After hundreds of metres of sustained cramponing Roger moves up to a ledge for one of our essential and regular tea stops.

SHISHAPANGMA (continued)

We climbed unroped to the rock rib which we had agreed as the safest line but, as I started up the rocks, the others stayed on the ice. For some distance we shouted the merits of rock or ice. I remained on the rib, hoping that the rock would prove more interesting than monotonous and gruelling front-pointing on the ice. Eventually Roger joined me but, at this point, the rock above got too hard, so we moved back to join Alex in the now very exposed ice couloir.

(*right*) A view down the initial ice couloir from the rock rib. (*below*) Alex's view of Roger and me moving into the couloir from the rib.

Completing a rock pitch and searching for a bivouac site at sunset.

Alex and Roger following a mixed pitch on the rock band.

We eventually made our first bivouac on a snow shoulder.

After a traverse to the left we moved round and up a snow arête in a last desperate search for a bivouac site as the shadows lengthened.

SHISHAPANGMA (continued)

We progressed steadily towards the rock band and there spent hours working a route up ice runnels and rock walls, searching with increasing desperation for a bivouac site. Two hours after sunset we emerged onto a snow shoulder where we cut out a platform for the bivouac tent, having climbed 1500m from the foot of the face. We made tea and got to sleep at midnight.

Above the rock band the route followed a peapod-shaped couloir. We moved up steadily, making our second bivouac at 7800m. The following day we passed through the upper cleft and out onto the summit slopes with enough time to reach the main tops on the summit ridge. The descent down the South Ridge in deteriorating weather was arduous and a third bivouac dismal. There followed an interminable descent down 45° snow and ice slopes. Thus we brought our climb to a successful completion after four days of intense concentration and effort on a big and very lonely peak.

Coming out of the top of the peapod-shaped couloir on the morning of the third day.

On the summit ridge of Shishapangma.

On the Great Plateau of Tibet the Himalayan peaks can be easily reached by road compared with a two-week march to reach Everest from the south.

EVEREST, NORTH-EAST RIDGE, 1987

When I tackled Everest's unclimbed North-East Ridge it had already defeated three strong British expeditions. Its upper part, approached from the North Col had, of course, been attempted by the pre-war Everesters and was finally climbed by the Chinese. But it was the pinnacled section below this that had stopped recent attempts, combined with the ridge's exposure to winds and storms.

Our cosmopolitan party comprised Nick Kekus, Rick Allen and Sandy Allan, all of whom had taken part an attempt in 1985, Steve Sustad (US), Robert Schauer (Austria), Sharu Prabhu (India), my son Michael with his fiancée Eva Jansson, and the brothers Sila and Nima Tamang.

After acclimatising in Nepal we loaded our equipment onto two Chinese lorries at the Tibetan border. The drivers were arrogant and impervious to all requests to stop at

points of interest, so we took a wicked delight in their discomfort when one of the lorries got stuck in a river, even though our sugar, rice and flour were soaked. We got our first view of Everest from the summit of the devastated monastery at Xegar and, after a further day's drive to the roadhead, yaks carried our equipment up to Base Camp where there were five other expeditions, including a one-man North Face bid by the volatile Iranian Mischa Saleki.

Loading equipment onto the Chinese trucks.

Buddhist monks complete a pilgrimage to one of the few remaining monasteries.

The fortified monastery at Xegar that was destroyed in the Cultural Revolution. What an act of faith it must have been for such a poor country to have erected these impressive buildings and we were appalled by the institutionalised vandalism which destroyed them, leaving the beautiful Buddhist murals open to the elements.

Prayer flags now proliferate at the summit of the Xegar monastery.

The lorry stalled in the Rongbuk river.

Yaks carrying equipment to Base Camp.

The North Face of Everest viewed across the ridge
used by all the pre-war attempts. The First
and Second Steps are on the left skyline and the West
Ridge and Hornbein Couloir are on the right.

The lower section of the North-East Ridge from the side of the East Rongbuk Glacier. The two lower rock steps are above the figure (not to be confused with the more famous steps just below the summit) and the difficult pinnacled section dominates the middle of the ridge.

Rick Allen and I approaching the first rock step.

Nick Kekus trying to locate the entrance to the snow cave at 7090m.

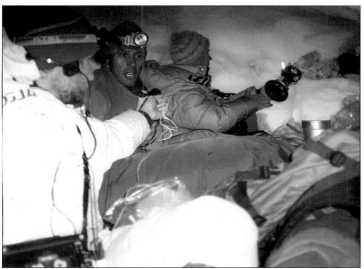

(*above*) Rick Allen approaching the wind-blasted ridge at 7500m above the rock steps and (*left*) recording a discussion with Robert Schauer in the first snow hole while Sandy Allan cooks.

EVEREST, NORTH-EAST RIDGE (continued)

It soon became clear that there was too much wind and too much snow for a realistic chance of success. We dug snow holes at 7090m and 7900m on the ridge and made a token attempt on the First Pinnacle, reaching a height of 8100m. Our second attempt was foiled by the wind and biting cold. One gust picked me bodily off my stance. We knew we would never be able to erect our small bivouac tent among the rocks above, so we retreated to Base where the expedition was brought to a premature end by a huge snowfall.

Rick Allen fighting wind and cold at 8000m above our final snow hole and (*below*) bracing against the wind near our high point at 8100m, half-way up the First Pinnacle.

(*above*) At Base Camp after the snowfall – a visiting cyclist's bike beleaguered. (*below*) Searching for Nima's body.

The view from the North-East Ridge of Everest east to Chomo Lonzo and Makalu in the middle distance and Kangchenjunga on the horizon.

EVEREST, NORTH-EAST RIDGE
(continued)

During the storm Sila and Nima had remained at Advance Base and they took the first opportunity to descend. On the trail by the East Rongbuk Glacier they were hit by an avalanche and Nima was buried. This was a bitter tragedy, all the more so as the accident had been in such a normally safe place. After a search we extricated his body and took it down to the Rongbuk Monastery. This had been pillaged by the Chinese but there were now a few monks and nuns in residence. The Head Lama had spent his years of exile in Nima's village in Nepal and it was thus fitting that he should give the last rites to my friend and companion on many expeditions.

Monks consult ancient texts before the funeral.

Rongbuk Monastery with Everest in the background – the scene for Nima's cremation.

The Taktsang Monastery.

The Taktsang (Tiger's Nest) Monastery that clings to the granite hillside 700m above the Paro Valley has become the symbol of Bhutan — a visual metaphor for its cautious isolationism and fastidious Buddhism. Taktsang is a shrine to Padma Sambhava or the Guru Rimpoche (Precious Teacher) who is credited with bringing Buddhism to both Tibet and Bhutan, arriving at Taktsang on a flying tiger.

There are only 1.3 million people in a country the size of Switzerland. It is one of the poorest countries in the world, but its subsistence farmers grow enough for their needs, and the country has an obvious balance and stability, though in the south there are now growing tensions with the Nepali community. Everywhere we met smiling faces and hospitality. The children who walked beside us did so out of curiosity or to practise their English which is taught in all Bhutanese schools. They did not ask us for anything.

Our objective was the unclimbed Jitchu Drake in the north-west corner of the country, close to the Indian and Tibetan borders. This had proved a difficult mountain, having taxed the energies of three previous expeditions. After a short period of sight-seeing around Paro, we acclimatised by a full circuit of the peak before choosing the South Face for our attempt.

The settlement around Ganty Monastery.

A rhododendron forest near Paro.

An old lady weaving the colourful cloth used for Bhutanese clothing.

(*top left*) Children peer through a fence – reflecting the caution of a country edging carefully into the modern world.

(*left*) A shrine in Thimphu built in memory of the much revered previous King of Bhutan.

(*below*) Well dressed school children in the village of Wangdiphodrang.

BHUTAN (continued)

Coming from Nottingham I was, of course, fascinated by the archery that is the national sport of Bhutan. It is taken very seriously and contests go on all day. A good shot is usually greeted with wild enthusiasm by team members and supporters. Correct dress is important – you can tell both a man's station in life and his home region by the style of his tunic.

(*below left*) Our team – myself, Victor Saunders, David Rose, Sharu Prabhu and Lindsay Griffin. (*below right*) The view east from Jitchu Drake to Kankar Punzum (7541m/24,734ft), one of the world's highest unclimbed peaks, but no longer accessible because the local headman complained to the King about disruptive large-scale expeditions.

The South Face of Jitchu Drake (6790m/22,227ft). The highest point is on the right beyond the South Summit. The Austrian expedition made a fine mixed route up the left-hand ridge in 1983 and in 1984 a Japanese party fixed ropes up the South-East Ridge on the right. We reached the ice shelf below this and then attacked the centre of the South Face before a violent snowstorm forced us off to high on the Japanese Ridge.

(*left and above*) I led steep ice pitches on the lower face that forcefully reminded me of the demands of technical climbing at altitude with the 'monkey on my back'. After the ice pitches the weather deteriorated and soon we were climbing with waves of snow pouring over us.

Victor Saunders leading up to the South Summit of Jitchu Drake with Chomolhari in the background. (*inset*) Victor and Sharu on the summit.

BHUTAN: JITCHU DRAKE (continued)

Lindsay was unwell so David offered to stay with him while Victor, Sharu and I went for the summit after a day's rest. We left at 2.30a.m. and after twelve pitches reached the South Summit, then moved on to the North Summit, gaining it at noon. The descent was sustained with many diagonal abseils and some hard down-climbing. It is one of the harder ice peaks I have climbed.

A photomontage of the summit of Jitchu Drake with satellite summits on the left and right. The Himalayan divide stretches 500 miles to the east to Burma and in that whole distance no more than two or three peaks have been climbed.

LADAKH: RIMO II, 1989

My expedition to the Rimo group of peaks of the eastern Karakoram proved to be one of the most frustrating ventures I have ever experienced. The mountain is in a war zone and has to be approached from India through Ladakh. Our permission dictated an Anglo-Indian expedition which had worked well with Balwant Sandhu on Shivling and Changabang but this time was rather less than satisfactory.

Our party comprised Rob Wood and his wife Laurie, Robert Schauer, Steve Sustad, Nick Kekus, Sharu Prabhu and myself. The Indian Army team was Sonam Palzor (leader), Tsewang Smanla, Kanhaiya Lal, Mohan Singh, plus a liaison officer, a doctor and a radio operator. It was this non-climbing rump that finally finished what might have been a very good trip.

For military reasons we had to spend three weeks waiting in Leh where, as forced tourists, we visited monasteries and Buddhist ceremonies. Eventually a military convoy took us over the Khardungla Pass (5585m/18,380ft) to Shyok and up the Nubra Valley which led to the Siachen Glacier. But the delay had been so long that Robert Schauer had to go home, soon to be followed by Rob Wood who had chest pains. Nearly a month after arriving in Leh we set up Base Camp below the Rimo group.

(*right and below*) At the Hemis Monastery in Leh:the monks with their haunting blend of wind and percussion accompany a drama to celebrate the birth of Padma Sambhava, he of the flying tiger in far away Bhutan.

Sonam Palzor, Sharu Prabhu, our liaison
officer and Kanhaiya Lal below Rimo II
with the rib and the couloir on the left.

We established ourselves at the head of the North Terong Glacier with an eye to the South Buttress of Rimo III (left). Before that we needed a joint climb for which we selected the unclimbed Rimo II (7373m/24,190ft). The Indian team decided to climb to the col between III and II while our group opted for the safer but harder rib to its right, above which we hoped to combine to climb Rimo II.

Nick Kekus and Steve Sustad led the rib, followed by Sharu, Laurie and me. The climbing was mixed and sustained, but safe. We reached the ridge above the col at the end of the second day. Laurie (severe headache) and Sharu were unable to continue, so I stayed with them while Nick and Steve pressed on to the summit. The Indians opted for a second ascent of the Rimo IV.

Rimo II from the North Terong Glacier. We climbed the slanting rib right of the col and then up the ridge to the summit. The Indian climbers went directly to the col and then across a snow basin beyond to climb Rimo IV.

An early morning view to the north-west to the peaks of the Gasherbrum group and K2.

12 Globetrotting

If two major Himalayan expeditions are undertaken each year life back home becomes pretty hectic. Is there not a conundrum here that every Himalayan regular must address at some time or other? The lure of the hills intensifies to escape the chaos at home that going to the hills brought about in the first place.

Happily, on a foreign lecture tour or while attending one of the many international mountaineering conferences and seminars, a quick climbing fix can often be built in. These gatherings are a great way to catch up with old friends and collect some unexpected gems along the way. In Australia I shared the enthusiasms of John Fantini for Bungonia, Rick White for Frog Buttress and Chris Baxter for all the crags in Victoria. There is a wealth of new lines for the taking, from Tasmania (Australia's best kept secret according to Jimmy Duff), to West Cape Howe, south of Perth, or King's Canyon near Alice Springs.

Every two years the Indian Mountaineering Foundation holds a conference at which climbers from all over the world meet up and have a chance to discover there is more to Indian climbing than the Himalaya, particularly in areas like the Western Ghats and further south, around Bangalore in Karnataka. The opportunity to go south came in 1986 after a conference at Manali when Sharu Prabhu and I joined Harish Kapadia's Bombay rock climbing group for a visit to the Sahyadri in the Western Ghats.

The Ghats are a worn and ancient land. Remnants of past glories abound with hill forts and temples and exotic black rock pinnacles. Even in November the rock is blistering hot and often loose because of the monsoon downpour and the heat on the volcanic rock. There are thirty-metre high crags only two hours from Bombay but it is worth travelling a greater distance to such places as Harihar Fort, built on the top of a triangle of sheer rock reached by a hewn staircase winding up through a hole in an overhang to the temple on top where the Diwali festival was being celebrated. On one side of this plug of rock there is an obvious 200m corner crack and chimney which was the hardest rock climb I did in India.

All over India there are walking and climbing clubs springing up,

Sharu climbing one of the flared chimney/groove lines typical of the Ramanagram Crags.

Approaching one of the main domes of the Ramanagram Crags. In October and November conditions for climbing are excellent. The granite cliffs offer a range of 5a–5c crack and groove lines with laybacking, jamming and off-width chimney climbing, all on good rock with excellent friction and variable protection and, as yet, happily, no bolts.

particularly around Bombay and Calcutta and local climbers have all the enthusiasm that I recall from my youth – cycling out to the crags with home-made equipment, or cast-off Western expedition gear bought from the bazaars of Kathmandu. Against all the odds, in isolation, with very little financial resources, the southern climbers have put up some impressive routes and mostly in good style.

We headed south. On the bus from Bombay to Bangalore Sharu and I spotted mile after mile of clean, hard unclimbed granite domes. At Bangalore, local climbers Mohan and Raju provided an introduction to Ramanagram where *A Passage to India* was filmed and some rock desecrated by having the Marabar Caves blasted into it. A temple by a lake in the rocks provided a bivvy and a base to climb flared and off-width cracks and chimneys, mostly two-pitch climbs, all hard but always on good rock.

This area between Bangalore and Mysore is in total contrast to the Western Ghats. The vegetation is far more luxuriant and, because there is not much tourism, local people show a natural curiosity and friendliness.

In 1987 I flew from a wet winter March in Cumbria to Amman with my daughter Martha, meeting Sharu there for two weeks' climbing in Jordan organised for us in the Wadi Rum by my friend Tony Howard. T. E. Lawrence had walked down Wadi Rum commenting that 'The Arab armies would have

Musical accompaniment for a Hindu festival in Kulu.

been lost in the length and breadth of it and within the walls a squadron of airplanes could have wheeled in formation.' He described the rock walls 'built sectionally, in crags like gigantic buildings along the two sides of their street. Deep valleys, fifty feet across, divided the crags, whose planes were smoothed by the weather into huge apses and bays, and enriched with surface fretting and fracture-like design.'

It was on this rock that we put up five new routes up to 450m in length. Tony pointed the way and Bernard Domenech from Chamonix joined Sharu, Martha and me on a long series of chimneys and stepped ledges, and on another route we had an unplanned and very cold bivouac in shorts and T-shirts.

In complete geographical contrast I also revisited the Arctic. I had only previously visited Baffin Island. Now in the late eighties I was lured to climbing areas in Iceland and Greenland and also did some winter climbing on the magnificent frozen waterfalls and ice sheets of Norway. The fine rock spires around Tasermuit Fjord in Greenland provided ample inspiration for future projects, while in Iceland I joined up with local climbers to make a number in interesting forays on ice and rock, the best of which were the columnar cliffs of Borgarhafnarfjall which I did with Snaevarr Gudmundsson.

Twice in the eighties I was invited to attend what can only be described as ice climbing master classes in Italy and Austria where I met the dynamic French alpinist and rock climber Thierry (Turbo) Renault with whom I seized the chance to do a fine vertical ice route. The British contingent on this meet were asked to demonstrate our typical mixed winter climbing, a style hardly practised in Europe at that time, despite obvious potential on the valley walls.

With my son Michael. We made an alpine-style ascent of Minipin (Diran) together in 1985.

While there is a special pleasure in pioneering routes in out of the way places, once you have experienced the Himalaya you are always lured back to that region of major set piece climbing. It was not until 1985 I visited Hunza and Nanga Parbat. With my son Michael and a couple of friends we made the first alpine-style ascent of the original route on Minipin in two days, with splendid views of Rakaposhi.

After this we went on to try Hanns Schell's route on the Rupal Face of Nanga Parbat, perhaps the most straightforward line of ascent up this highly complex and dangerous mountain. Believing we were fully acclimatised, Nazir Sabir, Michael, Alastair Reid and I tried for a rapid alpine-style push, but Alastair who was only on his first Himalayan visit began to suffer from altitude sickness, so we had to descend. This lends weight to the theory that acclimatisation is something one builds up from season to season, as well as by making acclimatising ascents at the start of each trip.

The Rupal flank of Nanga Parbat therefore represents fascinating uncompleted business and I look forward to a return visit.

Among this assembly are climbers (*front row, l to r*) H. P. S. Ahluwalia, D. K. Khullar, politician, myself, two politicians, Ed Hillary, M. S. Kohli, Junko Tabei, politician, Joginder Singh, Ad Carter, Jim Morrissey, Nawang Gombu, Mike Westmacott; (*back row*) Balwant Sandhu (5th from the left) and Peter Hillary (3rd from right).

INDIA

Assorted international climbers and notables convened for a mountaineering conference in Darjeeling in 1985. These events draw attention to the trekking and mountaineering in India with, paradoxically, a strong emphasis on environmental protection. Those who have climbed Everest and other 8000m summits are thought to have something significant to say. Afterwards I took the opportunity to visit some of India's better rock-climbing areas.

(*below left*) A flared chimney that we climbed at Ramanagram. (*below right*) On one of the sandstone slabs near the summit of Mount Abu in Rajasthan I did this sparsely protected HVS climb with the Barodan Praful Mistry and a passing Australian climber. (*inset*) Polo Ground Crag in Delhi.

A classic Frog Buttress crack climb (18).

(*left*) A sandstone climb (21) at King's Canyon — laybacking, with a fierce off-width finish.

Dennis Kemp and Lydia Brady at Arapiles. Lydia, who led Thunder Crack (24) after us, later soloed Everest from the South Col, without oxygen.

During visits to Australia I climbed on
Frog Buttress, renowned for its crack
climbs, and the celebrated Mount
Arapiles where I often teamed up with
the veteran English climber Dennis
Kemp. He had moved to Australia to
enjoy the ultimate climbing retirement,
but he sadly died in 1990 in a freak
belaying accident. With Rick White,
Sharu and I made a number of new
routes on the crags and canyons
around Alice Springs. Also of interest
were several fine sea cliffs, notably
West Cape Howe near Perth, which
offers five miles of magnificent granite
crack climbing. The finer grained
granite cliffs of Tasmania, provide a
different flavour of climbing that is no
less interesting.

Jim Duff (1975 Everest doctor) had emigrated to Tasmania. From his yacht he had spied scores of
lines on the sea cliffs around the island, including this excellent two-pitch groove climb (21).

Simon Yates and I on a new crack climb (24) on the fabulous granite cliffs of West Cape Howe, south of Perth.

Bedouin police patrol the cliffs of Wadi Rum.

JORDAN

The sandstone jebels of the Jordanian desert, north and east of Aqaba, are famed in the writings of T. E. Lawrence and others. Wadi Rum is of particular interest for climbers and has also spawned Bedouin experts who, while hunting, have developed a surprising climbing ability. The mountains are extensive sandstone blocks, up to 400m in height, criss-crossed by slit-like water-eroded canyons and embellished with wind-eroded arches and colonnades. The cool shade of the canyons contrasts with the glare of the desert, with pools of crystal clear sweet water fringed by the rich greens of ferns and lichen. This is the unique setting for some excellent rock climbing, using cracks and sculpted features on the walls for the most part eroded down to solid state.

(*far right*) We did five new routes during our visit, including a 500m crack and chimney climb with this fierce 5c crack at the start.

A Bedouin guide explaining Nabatean carvings.

Wind erosion has created this fine natural arch.

Thierry Renault following the first pitch and (*below*) leading the second pitch of our route.

AUSTRIA, 1986

International ice climbers gathered near Kitzbühel to highlight the potential of the frozen waterfalls of Austria. The delegates listened to talks with slides, and watched us climb. They were intrigued to learn of Mick Fowler's chalk climbs (with ice techniques) on the Dover cliffs, and stunned by two amazing lobs by Andy Nisbet. I did a variation on The Glass Madonna (*right*) with Thierry Renault, and a hard mixed line (*below*) with the Austrian, Andy Orgler, who later became an avid devotee of Scottish winter climbing.

(*above*) Helgi on the initial ice cliff and (*below*)
I thrash a way up the ice of the summit cliff.

Hrutsfjallstindar (1875m) stands in an arresting
position on the edge of the enormous Vatnajokull
Icecap in the south-east of the island. In 1986 I
joined IAC climbers Snaevarr Gudmundsson,
Thorstein Gudjonsson, Helgi Benediktson and
Jon Geirsson to make a 1400m TD climb up its
South-West Face (*left*). This linked a series of ice
columns. We based ourselves in an snow hole
below the first column (*insets left*) and climbed
the route the following day. The final column of
fragile, feathery ice gave a very serious pitch.

The Gullfoss waterfall, though just 32m high, debouches a massive melt water volume from the Langjokull icecap.

Strokkur geyser going through three stages of build-up.

ICELAND AND GREENLAND

The three-hundred member Icelandic Alpine Club has a core of active ice and rock climbers who are steadily advancing standards. The island has much to interest skiers, climbers, cavers, and geographers. With a highest peak of 2119m, four extensive icecaps and many glaciers, constant volcanic activity, hot springs, geysers and many spectacular waterfalls. I have David Oswin to thank for pushing me to go there, organising flights, a lecture date, and climbing partners, and I was so struck by this island of ice and fire that I have now been five times.

From the summit of Hrutsfjallstindar we were rewarded with a fabulous view across the icecap to Hvannadalshnukur (2119m/6950ft), Iceland's highest peak.

(*left*) With Snaevarr Gudmundsson I made the first new route (120m, E2) on Fallastakkanof, a fine basalt cliff with considerable potential. Icelandic rock climbing takes place mainly on a handful of such cliffs, but the locals are well placed for forays to Greenland with its immense potential for big-wall climbing. On a brief visit to Tasermuit Fjord near Kap Farvel in 1990 I studied its stately peaks and walls, including Apostelens Tommelfinger (*above*) and Suikkarsuak North (*below*). Bernard Amy who made routes here with other French climbers deliberately left no record, hoping that the region would become a preserve where each could experience the enjoyment of making his own new routes rather than following in the footsteps of others.

HUNZA/NANGA PARBAT 1986

Access to the Hunza region is now greatly eased by the Karakoram Highway. In 1986, taking advantage of this, a large team gathered with major ascents planned in several areas. But the best laid schemes were to be frustrated by excessive heat, illnesses and porter troubles.

We headed first for the fine rock pinnacle of Bubli-Mo-Tin or Lady's Finger, a satellite of Ultar (7388m). Greg Child, Sean Smith, Mark Miller, Steve Sustad and I climbed a long and dangerous couloir to the base of the pinnacle but here we were so tormented with diarrhoea that we had to withdraw after one minor ascent.

(*right*) Climbing the couloir below Bubli-Mo-Tin, weighed down with heavy loads for big-wall climbing.

(*bottom right*) Fit as butchers' dogs, Young Turks – Mark Miller (*left*), Snaevarr Gudmundsson, Steve Sustad and Alastair Reid.

(*below*) A photo stop on the Karakoram Highway, that now links Pakistan to Chinese Sinkiang.

The party moved to the Minipin Glacier where there was an ugly altercation with fifty-one Nagar porters demanding extortionate sums which we were compelled to pay. Seven Nagars were later arrested and disciplined for this exchange.

Our best climb here was a two-day alpine-style ascent of Minipin or Diran (Mark Miller, Alastair Reid, my son Michael and I, and Helgi Benediktsson, who completed the climb a day later). We then moved to attempt Nanga Parbat where, from Rupal Peak, we were able to study the Rupal Face – noted as the biggest precipice in the Greater Himalaya. Though none of us was very well, Nazir Sabir, Alastair Reid, Michael and I decided to attempt the South-West Ridge of Nanga Parbat but at a height of about 7350m Alastair fell ill (possibly a mild oedema) so we made an immediate retreat.

(*left*) The elegant 1000m pinnacle of Bubli-Mo-Tin (Lady's Finger) with the buttress on the right leading up to Ultar. We approached up the couloir on the left.

(*below*) Nagar porters carry loads on the tortuous path leading up to the Minipin Glacier.

(*below*) Nagar porters surround expedition members demanding twice the normal payment. Knowing that trekkers had been murdered in similar circumstances we paid up but seven porters were later arrested and faced floggings and a six-month prison term before we interceded.

Passing below a sérac wall on Minipin (Diran).

On the South-West Ridge of Nanga Parbat at about 7000m

(*below*) The North-West Face of Minipin or Diran (7266m/23,840ft). The mountain was first climbed in 1968 by Austrians Hanns Schell, Rainer Goschl and Rudolf Pischinger by a route rising diagonally from the basin on the left to the col on the West Ridge (right) which was then followed to the summit. Taking the same line we climbed the mountain in two days. The route was ideal for training being high enough for acclimatisation but not too hard.

The Rupal Face of Nanga Parbat.

Postscript

Compiling this book kept bringing me back to the question of what my climbing is for, what does it mean, and why do I do it? Mallory's quip to a tiresome questioner may serve as an enigmatic justification for one big obsessive project, but it hardly explains continual years of climbing on high mountains when logic and personal safety, not to mention domestic pressures and responsibilities, all suggest that one should ease off.

At its finest moments climbing allows me to step out of ordinary existence into something extraordinary, stripping me of my sense of self-importance. It is a feeling that might be compared with the heightened sense of humility caused by a bereavement or divorce, or the euphoria that accompanies an escape from a life-threatening accident or recovery from a serious illness. After surviving a bout of typhus in Kathmandu, I emerged from high fever, born again to all and everything around me, but conversely, though I have experienced many punishing failures, no mountain has ever humbled me as much as going through a year of separation and divorce in 1989.

The advantage of taking the mountain path is that it is all so simple – there is only me and the mountain medium, and at the critical time of engagement no one is involved but myself (and companions who are there for their own equally complex reasons). At such moments I have experienced profound changes in my perceptions and sense of awareness – particularly during ascents of the highest mountains.

Above 7500 metres progress becomes very difficult and it is here that, once poised, the climber can move into a realm that confronts him with the serious questions. On Kangchenjunga, when we had made the decision to have one last try and found that the winds had eased, it was like the parting of the Red Sea – a brief and precious lull, granted only to us, when for a few hours we were able to advance to the top of that great peak and return unscathed. Shishapangma demanded three days of intense climbing with the reward of that ethereal walk along the summit ridge. But the climb with Dougal Haston to the summit of Everest left the most profound impression. We had set out late, carrying no bivouac gear, knowing that we might well be benighted on the descent, and yet neither of us was concerned. As we moved along the final ridge I experienced that curious out of body sensation where part of my mind, separated from my labouring self, gave me protective advice over my left shoulder. We tarried on the summit for nearly an hour to watch the sunset on a magically calm evening and then spent our night in the snow hole without mishap when all logic pointed to a savage price that would have to be paid.

The nature of this fascination may be better understood by the Eastern philosophies. The Tao that can be told is not the real Tao according to the ancient Chinese and the point of tiptoeing along some summit ridge, strung out above the clouds a million miles from home, cannot be adequately explained by me either. It is only by experience that a climber can know what it is that takes him beyond himself – to risk his life, to come alive in an environment where every step of the way is more difficult than the last, stripped of all but the basic necessities for survival, putting earthly life in the lap of the gods, and yet with the calm prescience that all will be well; climbing up beyond suffering, fear and ego; not knowing where it will end – maybe on the summit and, if not, then as long as it is at the limit of endurance, that will have been enough to satisfy the soul and liberate the spirit; to bring *it* all back home; to face up to daily life but now with renewed enthusiasm and objectivity until *it* is lost and becomes a distant memory, but always a reference point for what is possible.

Then once again it is back to cranking up the energy to face officialdom, fund-raising, travelling out and walking in; to stake my life again, strapped to the mast like Ulysses, questing for that hidden treasure on those shimmering islands in the sky.

Climbing Record

Symbols * *first ascent* *w *first winter ascent* # *Himalayan alpine-style.*

1953 Black Rocks *Derbyshire* (Clive Smith, Terence Sterney) – first leads. Thereafter regularly walking and climbing in the Peak.

1955/6 Climbs on Ogwen cliffs *Snowdonia* (Mick Garside). Climbing instructor at Whitehall Centre.

1957 South Ridge Direct *Cir Mhor* (Mick Garside, Gordon Mansell, Maureen and Harold Drasdo) – first lead of a long mountain route.

1958 Winter circuit of Glen Nevis. First alpine season (Wes Hayden, Geoff Stroud) – glaciers/passes near Blümlisalp; Boeuf Couloir, Aig. du Peigne – attempt ended with 25m fall. Hitch-hiked to Yugoslavia.

1959 Voie des Plaques on Dent du Requin, Gouter Route on Mont Blanc (Des Hadlum); Cenotaph Corner, Cemetery Gates Snowdonia (Des Hadlum).

1960 Four-day Dauphiné circuit over Pic Coolidge, Dôme de Neige and Barre des Écrins (Lyn Noble, Mark Hewlett). Hitch-hiked to Morocco.

1961 North-East Face of Piz Badile (Des Hadlum). Guided for M.A. on eleven routes around Chamonix. Met Bonington and Whillans on Mont Blanc.

1962 East Face of Grand Capucin (Lyn Noble), Mer de Glace Face of Cornes des Chamois* (Ray Gillies). Atlas Mountains *Morocco* (Steve Bowes, Ray Gillies, Clive Davies and Steve Read) – Toubkal, South-East Cracks of Tadaft n'Gou Imrlay* (Read) and Volcan Siroua.

1963 Began five years of new routing on Derwent Valley limestone – best climbs: Cataclysm*, Catastrophe Grooves*, Highlight*, Gangue Grooves* and Lone Tree Groove* (all with Steve Read) and Limelight* (A3) (Terry Bolger). Comici/Dimai *Tre Cime* (Bill Cheverst) and other Dolomite climbs.

1964 Grot* (Patrick Harris) and Main Overhang Direct* (Ray Gillies) – hard A4 and A3 aid climbs at Gordale Scar *Yorkshire*. West Face of Aiguille de Blaitiere (Will McLaughlin).

1965 Tibesti Mountains *Chad* – first expedition organised – Tarso Tieroko* by West Ridge (Ray Gillies) and North Face* (Clive Davies).

1966 Crowbar* (Bill Cheverst) and Syringe* (Ray Gillies) Anglesey – but overaided. Led schools/youth expedition to Cilo Dag *Kurdistan*.

1967 Hindu Kush expedition – South Face of Koh-i-Bandaka*# (Ray Gillies), East Face of Koh-i-Sisgeikh*# (Tony Watts). North Face of Aig. du Plan (Bill Cheverst). Big Overhang* (A4) *Anglesey* (Brian Palmer).

1968 Bonatti Pillar of Petit Dru (Dave Nicol).

1969 Three-year development of main face of Strone Ulladale *Outer Hebrides*: The Scoop* (A4) (Jeff Upton, Guy Lee, Mick Terry); Sidewinder (A5) (Lee); The Nose* (A5) (Lee, Dennis Hennek). North Face Direct (Bauer/Rudolf) *Cima Ovest* (Upton, Ted Wells) – an early ascent.

1970 Rimmon Route (Guy Lee and Ted Wells), Hoibakk's Chimney (Terry Bolger), South-East Cracks, Adelsfjell (Wells) – *Romsdal*. Steck/Salathé Route on the Sentinel (Royal Robbins, Tony Willmott); Salathé Wall, El Capitan (Peter Habeler) first European ascent; South Face of BHOS Dome (Dennis Hennek, Don Lauria, T M Herbert).

1971 Spanish Route on Tosal de Malo *Pyrenees* (Dave Marriot). Baffin Island trip – East Face of Killabuk* (Dennis Hennek, Rob Wood, Ray Gillies, Steve Smith) and North Face of Breidablik (Hennek and Wood).

1972 Two attempts on the South-West Face of Everest *Nepal* – on Herrligkoffer expedition reached 8000m and on post-monsoon Bonington expedition reached 8300m (Dougal Haston, Mick Burke). East Pillar* of Mount Asgard *Baffin Island* (Dennis Hennek, Paul Nunn, Paul Braithwaite).

1973 The Nose, El Capitan (Rick White) – 65% free with aid mainly on nuts.

1974 Changabang* *India* (Martin Boysen, Chris Bonington, Dougal Haston, Tashi Chewang, Balwant Sandhu). South East Ridge*# of Pic Lenin *Pamirs* (Clive Rowland, Guy Lee, Paul Braithwaite). South Face of Midi (Paul Braithwaite) and Couturier Couloir of Verte (large party) during winter Everest training session.

1975 Ogre Reconnaissance *Pakistan* (Clive Rowland, Rob Wood, Ronnie Richards). South-West Face* of Everest *Nepal* (Dougal Haston) – expedition led by Chris Bonington. Little Wing *Yosemite* – at 5.10d my hardest rock lead.

1976 South Face Diagonal*# of Denali *Alaska* (Dougal Haston). South-West Buttress of Overlord* *Baffin Island* (Dennis Hennek). Diamond Lil*, Long's Peak *Colorado* (Dennis Hennek, Mike Covington). North-East Face* of Nelion and Diamond Couloir *w Mount Kenya (Paul Braithwaite).

1977 The Ogre or Baintha Brakk* by the West Ridge *Pakistan* (Chris Bonington plus Clive Rowland and Mo Anthoine to final tower).

1978 South-East Chimney of Mount Waddington *Canada* (Rob Wood) with walk-in from sea-level. West Ridge of K2 *Pakistan* – Chris Bonington's expedition curtailed after Nick Estcourt's death. North Ridge of Nuptse# *Nepal* (Mike Covington, Joe Tasker) – abandoned after heavy snow fall.

1979 North Ridge* of Kangchenjunga *Nepal* (Joe Tasker, Pete Boardman). First lightweight ascent of a new route one of the Big Three. North Summit*# of Kusum Kangguru *Nepal* (Georges Bettembourg). North Buttress* of Nuptse *Nepal* (Al Rouse, Brian Hall, Georges Bettembourg) – # from Western Cwm. The Smear *Skye* *w (Jim Duff).

1980 North-East Spur of Les Droites (Adrian Burgess) – third winter ascent. Two alpine rock climbs*, Darrens *New Zealand* (Jim Duff, Merv English, Arianne Giobellina). West Ridge of K2 *Pakistan* (Pete Boardman, Joe Tasker, Dick Renshaw) attempt abandoned after tactical wrangles. South-East Ridge of Makalu# *Nepal* (Georges Bettembourg, Roger Baxter-Jones) – a nine-day climb. We reached 8180m where Bettembourg became ill. Training climbs included a variation finish to the Original Route on Kangchungste#.

1981 East Pillar*# of Shivling *India* (Rick White, Greg Child, Georges Bettembourg) – a thirteen-day climb. North Face of P.7010*# of Chamlang, *Nepal* (Reinhold Messner, Pasang Mingma, Ang Dorje).

1982 North Face of Monte Gruetta (Roger Baxter-Jones, Alan Rouse) – winter attempt. South-East Face* of Shishapangma and Pungpa Ri*# by the South-East Face *Tibet* (Roger Baxter-Jones, Alex MacIntyre).

1983 Expedition to Baltoro/K2 area *Pakistan*: Lobsang Spire*# by South Pillar (A3) Pakistan (Greg Child, Pete Thexton); Original Route on Broad Peak# (Steve Sustad); South Pillar of K2# (Andy Parkin, Roger Baxter-Jones, Jean Afanassieff) – retreated when Afanassieff became ill at 7500m practically at the Shoulder.

1984 Barun Valley *Nepal*: Acclimatised on Yaupa South-East (6300m)*# and Baruntse#. Chamlang East* and Central* by East Ridge, descending North Face*# (Michael Scott, Ang Phurba, Jean Afanassieff); South-East Ridge of Makalu# (Steve Sustad, Afanassieff) – at 8370m Afanassieff called retreat. Orion Face, the Curtain and Green Gully *Ben Nevis* (with Jim Fullalove but unroped).

1985 Minipin# *Pakistan* (Michael Scott, Mark Miller, Alastair Reid) – two-day ascent, and climbed to 7400m on South-West Ridge of Nanga Parbat*# (Nazir Sabir, Scott and Reid) where illness to Reid forced retreat.

1986 South-East Face Direct* of Mount Colonel Foster *Canada* (Greg Child, Rob Wood). Waterpipe Gully *w *Skye*, Route left of Y Gully *w *Applecross*, Captain Patience *w *Seanna Bhraigh* (all with Colin Downer). South Face* of Hrutsfjallstinder (Snaevarr Gudmundsson, Helgi Benediktsson, Jon Geirsson and Thorsteinn Gudjonsson) and Organ Pipes*, Fallastakkanof *Iceland* (Benediktsson). Rock climbs* in Western Ghats, Ramanagram and Savandurga *India* (Sharu Prabhu, Praful Mistry, Dhiren Toolsidas, D. V. Ruckmangada Raju and K. V. Mohan).

1987 Rock climbs* in Wadi Rum *Jordan* (Martha Scott, Sharu Prabhu and Bernard Domenech). East Face of K2# *Pakistan* – attempt failed, heavy snow. North-East Ridge of Everest# *Nepal* – to 8200m (Rick Allen) – attempt failed, high winds.

1988 Ice climbs in Norway – South Side* of Hemsedal (Stein Aasheim and another); Blomannen Face* and other routes, Lyngen Peninsula (Sjur Nessaieim). Jitchu Drake*# by South Face *Bhutan* (Victor Saunders, Sharu Prabhu). West Face of Makalu *Nepal* – attempt failed, bad weather.

1989 Rimo II, East Karakoram *India* reached 6660m# (with Sharu Prabhu and Laurie Wood). Peak climbed*# by Steve Sustad and Nick Kekus. Rock routes* in King's Canyon and West Cape Howe *Australia* (Rick White, Sharu Prabhu, Simon Yates, Rowland Tyson).

1990 The Indian Arete*# on Latok 3 *Pakistan* (Sandy Allan) – 800m TD sup.

1991 Hanging Glacier Peak South (6294m)*# by the South Ridge, Kanjiroba Himal *Nepal* (Sharu Prabhu, Nigel Porter) – a TD mixed climb.

Bibliography Detailed accounts in books (* indicates other authors): *Everest, South West Face** (Hodder, 1973), *Big Wall Climbing* (Kaye and Ward, 1974); *Changabang* (Heinemann, 1975), *Everest the Hard Way** (Hodder, 1976), *The White Death** (Reymond, 1981), *Sacred Summits** (Hodder, 1982), *Savage Arena** (Methuen, 1982), *The Shishapangma Expedition* (Granada, 1984), *The Everest Years** (Hodder, 1986). Bound expedition reports: *Tibesti* (1965), *Cilo Dag* (1966), *Hindu Kush* (1967).

There are numerous magazine and journal accounts (by me and others) including: *Mountain Craft* 60, 71, 75; *Mountain* 3, 5, 7, 15, 22, 23, 26, 33, 34, 47, 52, 57, 77, 84, 93, 99, 100, 101, 111, 125; *Climbing* 112; *Alpine Journal* 319, 322, 324, 326, 327, 331, 335–338; *American Alpine Journal* 46–47, 49–65 (the main information source for expeditions).

Photography Up to 1967 I used an Ilford Sportsman. Then I bought a Pentax SLR from Pete Crew, and thereafter (with the exception of the expedition issue Olympus cameras on Everest in 1975) have always used Pentax cameras. My current equipment is an SLR Pentax LX, a compact Pentax 90mm zoom for lightweight action, and a Pentax 6x7 for larger format work.